Gandhi’s Vision

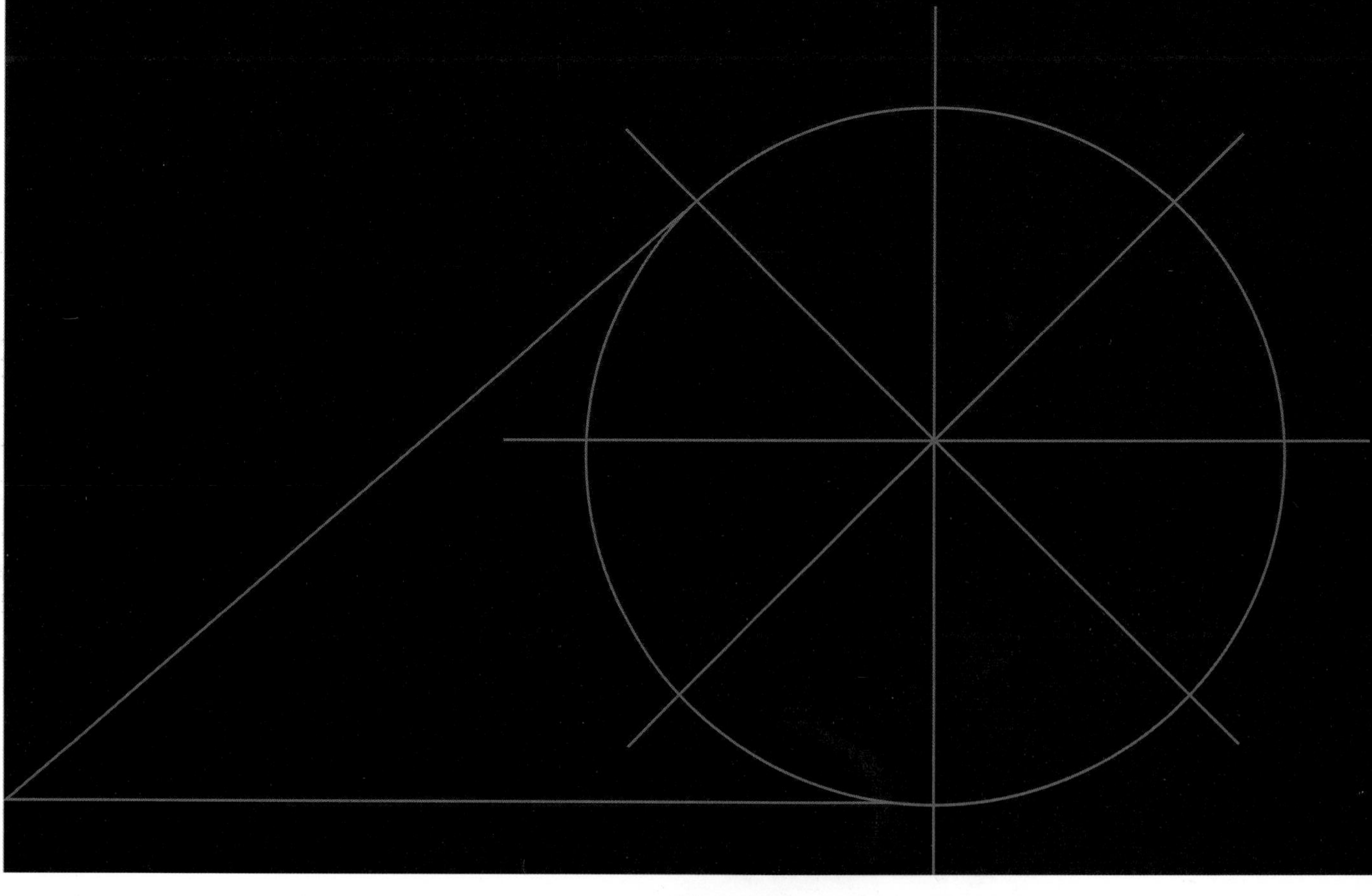

Gandhi's Vision
Freedom and Beyond

Aparna Basu

National Gandhi Museum
New Delhi

NIYOGI
BOOKS

A collaborative publishing effort between
National Gandhi Museum, Jawaharlal Nehru Marg, New Delhi-110002
and Niyogi Books, D-77, Okhla Industrial Area, Phase-1, New Delhi-110020

Published by
NIYOGI BOOKS
Block D, Building No. 77,
Okhla Industrial Area, Phase-I,
New Delhi-110 020, INDIA
Tel: 91-11-26816301, 49327000
Fax: 91-11-26810483, 26813830
Email: niyogibooks@gmail.com
Website: www.niyogibooksindia.com

Editor: Arunima Ghosh
Design: Misha Oberoi

ISBN: 978-93-85285-93-6
Publication: 2018
Reprint: 2025

Printed at: Niyogi Offset Pvt. Ltd., New Delhi, India

Contents

Gandhi with women workers during his visit to Lancashire, 1931

Introduction

The idea of this book originated with an exhibition organised by the National Gandhi Museum and the India International Centre, New Delhi, in August 2017 to commemorate 70 years of Indian independence. We decided that instead of depicting India's achievement since 1947, we would chronicle the main events leading to India's independence under Gandhi's leadership and his vision of a free India. The exhibition was widely appreciated and very favourably reviewed in the press. Niyogi Books expressed a wish to publish a book of the photographs with an enlarged accompanying text to coincide with the 149th birth anniversary of Mahatma Gandhi in 2018.

So much has already been written about Gandhi that one may well ask, is another book required? Commemorating national leaders is usually confined to eulogising their personality and achievements. We felt that what was necessary was a concerted effort to connect their actions and thought to problems and apprehensions of today's India. Among those stalwarts who led the freedom movement, Mahatma Gandhi shines not only for the novel means of non-violence, but also for simultaneously wanting to root out social evils like communal hatred, untouchability and gender disparity. With several such issues espoused by him continuing to dominate the social space, his teachings remain relevant today.

The first part of the book deals with the freedom struggle under Gandhi's leadership. In the history of national liberation struggles, India's freedom struggle led by Mahatma Gandhi occupies a unique position. The Indian national movement was one of the biggest mass movements in modern history. Gandhi understood that an effective struggle against alien rule must be based on the active participation of all the sections of society. When asked by a foreign journalist in 1942 as to how he hoped to make the British quit India, he replied 'With the might of the dumb millions.'[1] It is truly amazing how Gandhi mobilised people from all religions, regions and social groups across the country—Hindus, Muslims and Parsis, peasants and landlords, workers and capitalists, the intelligentsia and the illiterates, men and women, the young and the old.

In all other countries of Africa, South East Asia or Latin America, it was by armed revolts that oppressive foreign rule was overthrown. Gandhi believed in the moral superiority of non-violence. His concept of non-violent protest, emphasis on means as ends in themselves, 'double advocacy'—an idea that sees elements of truth in both sides of an argument, and above all, the insistence on the conversion of the opponent rather than coercion are recognised as valid and usable weapons in conflict situations. Gandhi laid stress on discussion, persuasion, dialogue, compromise, consensus and winning over the opponent, rather than on overt clashes. To search for areas of agreement that could produce settlement remained central to his technique.

'No idea has achieved an impact so far-reaching and so fundamentally humane as non-violence has.' (Ramin Jahanbegloo, 2018)[2]. Gandhi was admired by the African Americans in the USA as early as the 1920s. In 1936, Howard Thurman, a distinguished Baptist Minister and academic from the American South, led a delegation of prominent African Americans to India to meet Gandhi who explained to them his principles of non-violent resistance to injustice. Gandhi told them that 'it may be through the Negroes that the unadulterated message of non-violence will be delivered to the world.'[3] Gandhi inspired Baynard Rustin and Philip Randolph who together founded the Congress of Racial Equality in Chicago in 1942. In December 1955, an African American teacher, Rosa Parks refused to give up her seat on a crowded bus. She was arrested and charged with breaking the local segregation laws. When the court punished her with a fine of $14, civil rights workers protested by organising a boycott of the city's buses. Rustin came to Montgomery to work as an adviser to the campaign. He persuaded Martin Luther King Jr to embrace non-violence as the key element of the struggle. King had heard about Gandhi's role in the Indian freedom struggle but not much more. He acknowledged that his inspiration was Jesus Christ, but he learnt the method of his struggle from Gandhi.

In South Africa, non-violent protest and mass resistance played an important role in the fight against apartheid and white domination especially between 1950 and 1960. Nelson Mandela acknowledged how Gandhi's philosophy contributed in no small measure to bringing about a peaceful transformation in South Africa.

Solidarity (an anti-bureaucratic, civil resistence movement to advance the causes of workers' rights and social change) in Poland began in 1980 and concluded in 1989 with the collapse of the Communist regime. Lech Walesa, leader of the movement writes,

> I too consider myself a follower and student of Mahatma Gandhi... Until 1970, I had not believed that the methods of Mahatma Gandhi could be effective. I could not believe that the Soviet communist empire could be defeated by peaceful measures... It is true that in the 1940s and 1950s we tried to oppose the communist system with arms. We lost in these attempts...Finally following the example of Mahatma Gandhi we found that by adopting peaceful non-violent measures we could re-organise the society and empowered by the resulting solidarity and togetherness we could effectively lead the struggle. We did not lose this attempt.[4]

In 1968 and 1969, following the Warsaw Pact invasion, Czechs and Slovaks held off full soviet control for eight months with improvised non-violent struggle and refused collaboration. Victor Havel, the Czech statesman, called non-violence 'the power of the powerless.'[5]

Gandhi was one of twentieth century's transformative political leaders. Among his many contributions, he is rightly credited with pioneering *satyagraha*, resistance to tyranny and injustice by non-violent means. He wanted India to be free from foreign rule, but was convinced that only a powerful mass movement based on the principle of non-violence would be able to mobilise people throughout the country. His message resonated with the people of India. He was a pragmatist and realised that it was not possible to overthrow British rule by an armed revolt.

The book begins with the nineteenth century social and religious reform movements and Raja Rammohan Roy, often described as the Father of Modern India. These years saw the beginnings of a new political awakening. It then moves on to the Partition of Bengal and the Swadeshi movement and then to Annie Besant and the Home Rule League.

Gandhi evolved his technique of *satyagraha* in South Africa and his movements there succeeded. He returned to India in 1915 after spending over two decades in South Africa and on the advice of Gopal Krishna Gokhale toured round the country to understand the real India and familiarise himself with the condition of the poor and marginalised.

He launched three local *satyagraha*s in all of which he succeeded in achieving his objectives by non-violent means. In 1917 he launched his first *satyagraha* in India in the Champaran district of Bihar to help the peasants who were forced to grow indigo and treated very harshly by the planters. The next year, he was in Ahmedabad to settle the dispute between the textile workers and mill owners. And finally, a *satyagraha* was launched in the Kheda district of Gujarat to help the peasants who refused to pay taxes due to

Gandhi with his South African friends

severe famine. In each case, Gandhi agreed to intervene only after minutely studying the ground situation and making specific demands which had to be just. Before starting the *satyagraha* campaign in Bardoli, under Vallabhbhai Patel's leadership, a detailed survey was made of the *taluka* and months were spent in preparing the peasants, warning them of the consequences of a no-tax campaign. This phase is important as it depicts how after his success in South Africa, Gandhi tested his technique of *satyagraha* in India.

After his success at the local level, he was now ready to move to the national arena to launch the Rowlatt Satyagraha, the Khilafat/Non-Cooperation Movement, the Salt Satyagraha, the Civil Disobedience Movement and the Quit India Movement.

Gandhi spent the last two years of his life in Noakhali, Bihar and Calcutta trying to restore communal peace and harmony. On 15 August 1947, the architect of India's freedom was in Calcutta working for Hindu-Muslim unity.

The second part is on Gandhi's dream of free India. For Gandhi, freedom from foreign rule was not the end. It was the beginning of an effort to build a new India. It is amazing how his views on pluralism, untouchability, gender equality, cleanliness, environmental protection, an open society and polity are relevant even today.

Towards Freedom

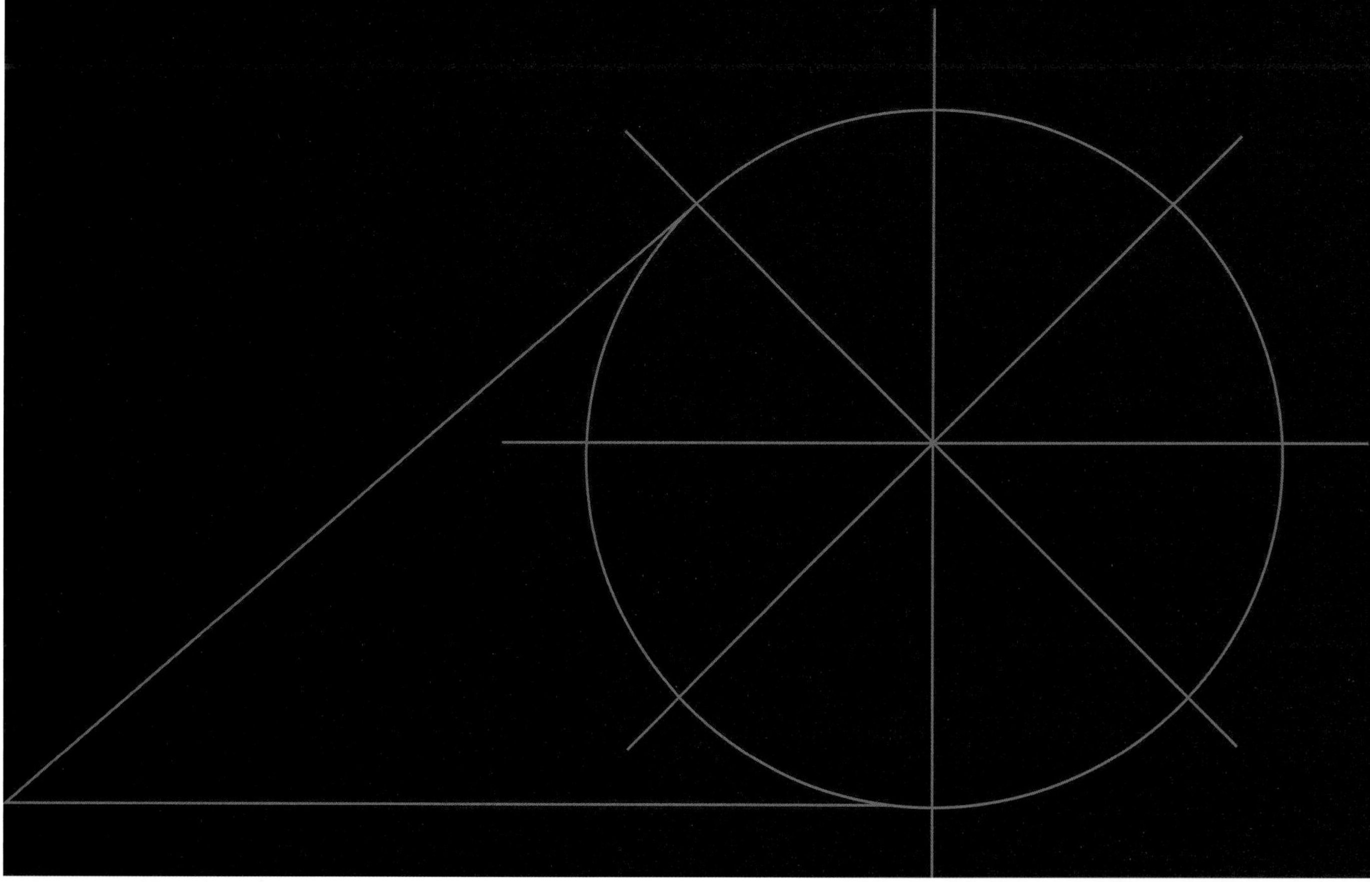

In the course of the nineteenth century, India underwent a remarkable transformation. There were social and religious reform movements, a literary renaissance and an awakening of patriotic feelings. The social reform movements began with individual revolts against particular social customs and religious practices which had always been a feature of Indian society, but they adopted Western methods of organisation and propagation. Political ideas and associations developed which contributed to the emergence of Indian nationalism.

At the Karachi Congress meeting, 1931

The Awakening

It is generally agreed that the Indian social reform movements of the nineteenth century grew out of the encounter with the West. The British conquest and the consequent dissemination of Western culture and ideology led to an introspection of the strengths and weaknesses of indigenous culture and institutions. As the East India Company's rule with its new agrarian and industrial relations expanded, together with the new administrative structure and introduction of English education, existing dominating groups such as the *zamindars*, scribes, traders, etc. began to be forged into a new middle class or urban intelligentsia. This class sought to reform itself initiating campaigns against caste, purdah, sati, child marriage, condition of widows, etc. seeing them as elements of pre-modern identity.

The reform movements emphasised not only humanitarian and spiritual equality, like the earlier *bhakti* movements, but also ideas of individualism, natural rights, duties of the individual to society and the possibility of progress. The special character of the nineteenth and twentieth century revolts lay in the fact that they originated from secular motives based on rational critiques of society and led to secular as well as religious movements for social reform; it spread to all parts of India; it was supported by the state which resulted in legislation and administrative action; and finally, it became an explicit or implied premise of all nationalist thoughts.

The spirit of reform, which embraced almost the whole of India, began with the efforts of Raja Rammohan Roy (1772–1833) in Bengal leading to the formation of the Brahmo Samaj in 1828. Apart from the Brahmo Samaj, the Prarthana Samaj in Maharashtra and Gujarat and the Arya Samaj in Punjab and North India were some of the prominent reform movements. There were several caste and regional movements also.

One of the striking trends of the Indian awakening was the growth of political consciousness whose origin can be traced to Rammohan Roy whose political writings on judicial reform, civil rights, the separation of powers, freedom of the press, and other liberal doctrines, became standard works for the political reform movements fifty years later. In 1823, the acting Governor General, Adam issued a Press Ordinance taking away the liberty of the press. Rammohan with a few of his associates submitted a memorial to the Supreme Court against the Ordinance and sent a petition to the King-in-Council. In his appeal Rammohan wrote: 'A free press has never yet caused a revolution in any part of the world' because, if grievances are articulated and redressed,

Raja Rammohan Roy (1772–1833)
A social and religious reformer, he founded the Brahmo Samaj in 1828 and advocated the abolition of *sati*

the grounds of discontent are removed. 'It is well known that despotic governments naturally desire the suppression of any freedom of expression which might tend to expose their acts of obloquy...'[6] His memorial was not accepted but as a mark of protest he discontinued the publication of the *Mirat-ul-Akbar*, in the last editorial of which he made a scathing attack on this objectionable decree.

Rammohan also opposed the Jury Act of 1827 which declared that henceforth Hindus and Muslims could be tried only by either European or native Christians, but no Christian, either European or native, could be tried by a Hindu or Muslim judge. Moreover, no Hindu or Muslim was to get a seat in the Grand Jury. Rammohan submitted a petition against the Act to both Houses of Parliament.

In 1830, he protested against government measures to tax rent free lands. He was against the monopoly rights enjoyed by the East India Company and one of the objects of his journey to England was to demand more rights and privileges for Indians at the time of the renewal of the Company's Charter in 1833. He submitted to the Select Committee of the British Parliament various demands including appointment of Indians in the Civil Service, trial by jury, consulting Indian public opinion before enacting legislation, etc. Though these demands were not conceded, and may appear to be narrow today, they have to be judged keeping in mind the time when he expressed them. These later became the demands of the pre-Gandhian nationalist movement.

The first generation students of Hindu College, referred to as 'Young Bengal', inspired by their teacher Vivian Derozio, continued the political agitation that started from the time of Rammohan. They were known for their patriotism and

LEFT TO RIGHT

M.G. Ranade (1842–1901)
A distinguished scholar, social reformer and author. A founding member of the Indian National Congress (INC); he was also a member of the Bombay legislative council, a member of the financial committee, and a judge of Bombay High Court

Pherozeshah Mehta (1845–1915)
A nationalist, 'moderate' and a founder member of the Congress, he formed the Bombay Presidency Association

LEFT TO RIGHT

Swami Vivekananda (1863–1902)
Disciple of Ramakrishna Paramhansa and founded the Ramakrishna Mission

Sri Aurobindo (1872–1950)
A philosopher, yogi, guru and a nationalist; he joined the Indian movement for independence from British rule, but is best known for his philosophy on human evolution and Integral yoga; founder of Sri Aurobindo Ashram Auroville

FACING PAGE

Kashinath Trimbak Telang (1850–1893)
Originator of the Bombay Presidency Association, besides Pherozeshah Mehta; he was the first secretary of the INC; an Indologist; and a judge at the Bombay High Court

advanced political thinking. They were influenced by Tom Paine, Gibbon, Bacon and ideas of the French Revolution.

In the second half of the nineteenth century, the social revolt became more intense and led to endeavours which were based on a concern for the progress of the nation. Keshab Chandra Sen (1838–1884), the leader of the Brahmo Samaj and its greatest missionary, dreamt of a great national awakening which would combine religious and social reform. 'What we see around us today,' he said, 'is a fallen nation—a nation whose primitive greatness lies buried in ruins.'[7]

Bombay was not far behind Calcutta in producing young rebels, chiefly the produce of the Elphinstone Institution founded in 1827 to promote English education, on the model of Hindu College. The Bombay Students' Literary and Scientific Society organised lectures on social and political issues.

In the mainstream of the national social reform movement in the 1880s in Bombay were Madhav Govind Ranade (1842–1901), Kashinath Trimbak Telang (1850–1893), Ramkrishna Gopal Bhandarkar (1837–1925) and Narayan Ganesh Chandavarkar (1855–1923). Ranade was one of the founders of the National Social Conference as well as of the Indian National Congress.

Between 1875 and 1885 a number of new associations were founded. The British India Association of Bengal became increasingly identified with the *zamindars* and thus lost its anti-British thrust. The Bombay Association and the Madras Native Association had also become redundant. And so the younger nationalists of Bengal led by Surendranath Banerjea and Ananda Mohan Bose, founded the Indian

Association in 1876. Political organisations in Bombay and Madras were also enlarging the base of their memberships and reaching out into small towns to strengthen their claim to represent popular opinion.

M. Viraraghavachariar, G. Subramaniya Iyer, P. Ananda Charlu and others formed the Madras Mahajan Sabha in 1884. In Bombay, Badruddin Tyabji, Pherozeshah Mehta, K.T. Telang and a few other like-minded persons broke away from older leaders like Dadabhai Framji and Dinshaw Petit, and formed the Bombay Presidency Association in 1885. The speeches and writings of Swami Vivekananda with his emphasis on the pride of being an Indian inspired many; so did the writings of Sri Aurobindo .

Another sign of the new political life in the country was the coming into existence during these years of nearly all the major nationalist newspapers which dominated the Indian national scene till 1918— *The Hindu*, *Tribune*, *Bengalee*, *The Mahratta* and *Kesari*. The one exception was the *Amrita Bazar Patrika* which had already been in publication in Bengali, but became an English language newspaper in 1878.

The nationalists felt the need for establishing an all India political association. They had gained confidence as a result of organising a large number of agitations in the preceding ten years. Since 1875 there had been campaigns around cotton import duties which Indians wanted to be retained in the interest of the Indian textile industry. Nationalists opposed the Afghan adventures of Lord Lytton. The Indian press had waged a campaign against the Vernacular Press Act which sought to control the press. A major agitation was launched in 1883 in favour of the Ilbert

Allan Octavian Hume (1929–1912)
Founder of the Indian National Congress,
came to India as an ICS officer

Bill which would enable Indian magistrates to try Europeans. Indians felt that their efforts had failed because they did not have an all India organisation. In 1885, A.O. Hume founded the Indian National Congress to give vent to the political aspirations of the newly emerging urban intelligentsia through speeches, petitions and articles. They asked for the greater participation of Indians in the government and the Civil Service while professing loyalty to the Raj.

Gandhi with women *satyagrahis*, South Africa

Pre-Gandhian Movements in India and Gandhi in South Africa

SWADESHI MOVEMENT

The Swadeshi movement was a result of the partition of Bengal by Lord Curzon in 1905. Conceived as an administrative readjustment of boundaries, it was overshadowed by political considerations. The movement formally began on 7 August at the historic Town Hall meeting in Calcutta, presided over by Maharaja Mahindra Chandra Nandi and addressed by Surendranath Banerjea. The protest took the form of boycott of foreign goods and the patronage of indigenous products popularly known as *swadeshi*. All classes of people—*zamindars*, professional groups such as lawyers, teachers, journalists, doctors, students and women joined the movement.

Rabindranath Tagore announced his plan in September 1905 to observe *raksha bandhan* on 16 October, the partition

Surendranath Banerjea (1848–1925)
A nationalist; participated in the Swadeshi movement;
edited *Bengalee*; was elected President of the Congress twice

LEFT TO RIGHT

Sarla Devi Chaudhurani (1872–1950)
Niece of Rabindranath Tagore. Fiery nationalist, editor of a women's magazine, *Bharati*, and the founder of the first All India Women's Association in India

Bipin Chandra Pal (1858–1932)
He was an 'extremist' and along with Lala Lajpat Rai and Bal Gangadhar Tilak, they became the 'Lal Bal Pal trio'

Sister Nivedita (1867–1911)
Disciple of Vivekananda. Originally known as Margaret (Margot) Elizabeth Noble, she was of Scottish-Irish origin

Bankim Chandra Chatterjee (1838–1894)
Author of numerous Bengali novels, including *Anand Math*; composed 'Bande Mataram'

day, and women took part in it. Another rite observed on this day was *arandhan*, suggested by Ramendrasundar Trivedi, asking women not to cook. Women organised *swadeshi bhandar*s and Sarala Devi Chaudhurani, niece of the Rabindranath Tagore, opened Lakshmi Bhandar which sold only *swadeshi* products. Women gave up using imported cloth and smashed their bangles (*churis*). Bipin Chandra Pal addressed women's meetings during his tour of East Bengal in 1907 and the women of Tangail gave a big reception to Surendranath Banerjea when he visited Mymensingh later that year. A women's meeting was organised in the house of the eminent physician Dr Nilratan Sircar to honour the revolutionary Bhupendranath Dutta's mother. A number of women in Barisal gave their savings to the Swadeshi Bhandar Samiti.

Secret societies had started earlier In Maharashtra, and in Bengal, revolutionary organisations began to develop, mainly owing to the efforts of Aurobindo Ghose. The most important of these was the Anusilan Samiti founded in 1897. It received active help and encouragement from Sister Nivedita . Among others connected with the growth of revolutionary societies were Barindra Ghose (brother of Aurobindo) and Sarala Devi Chaudhurani. Women circulated revolutionary leaflets and helped in maintaining liaison between different revolutionary leaders.

As the movement spread over Bengal, mass meetings were organised where the creed of *swadeshi* was preached. Bonfires of foreign goods were held and students boycotted government schools and colleges. 'Bande Mataram', the sacred *mantra* of Bankim Chandra, became the rallying cry and inspired people with a new sense of patriotism and

Annie Besant (1847–1933)
She was a socialist, theosophist, women's right activist and founder of the Home Rule League; she was the first woman president of the Indian National Congress

national consciousness. The president of the Indian National Congress, at its 1906 session held in Calcutta, expressed the demand for *swaraj*. Aurobindo Ghose declared the attainment of complete freedom as the goal of the national movement.

The demand for national education was also a part of the Swadeshi movement. National schools were started and a technical college was opened in Jadavpur. With the annulment of the Partition in 1911, the Swadeshi movement, which had been largely centred in Bengal, petered out.

THE HOME RULE LEAGUE, LOKMANYA TILAK AND ANNIE BESANT

Before Gandhi, Bal Gangadhar Tilak was the most widely known Indian political leader. Unike his contemporary Maharashtrian Gopal Krishna Gokhale, Tilak was a radical nationalist but conservative in his views on social reform. In 1897, plague broke out in Poona and the government had to undertake segregation and house search. Tilak organised his own relief measures, but criticized the government for its harsh measures. As a result, he was arrested under Section 124 A of the Indian Penal Code on the charge of sedition. He was once again arrested in 1908 on the charge of writing polemical articles intensifying racial animosity between Indians and the British. In June 1914, he was released after spending six years in prison, most of which he had spent in Mandalay in Burma.

On his return, he found the political situation in India very different. Aurobindo Ghose had given up politics for a spiritual life in Pondicherry. Lala Lajpat Rai was away in

Members of the Home Rule League with Annie Besant

FACING PAGE Gandhi with Annie Besant, Madras, 1921

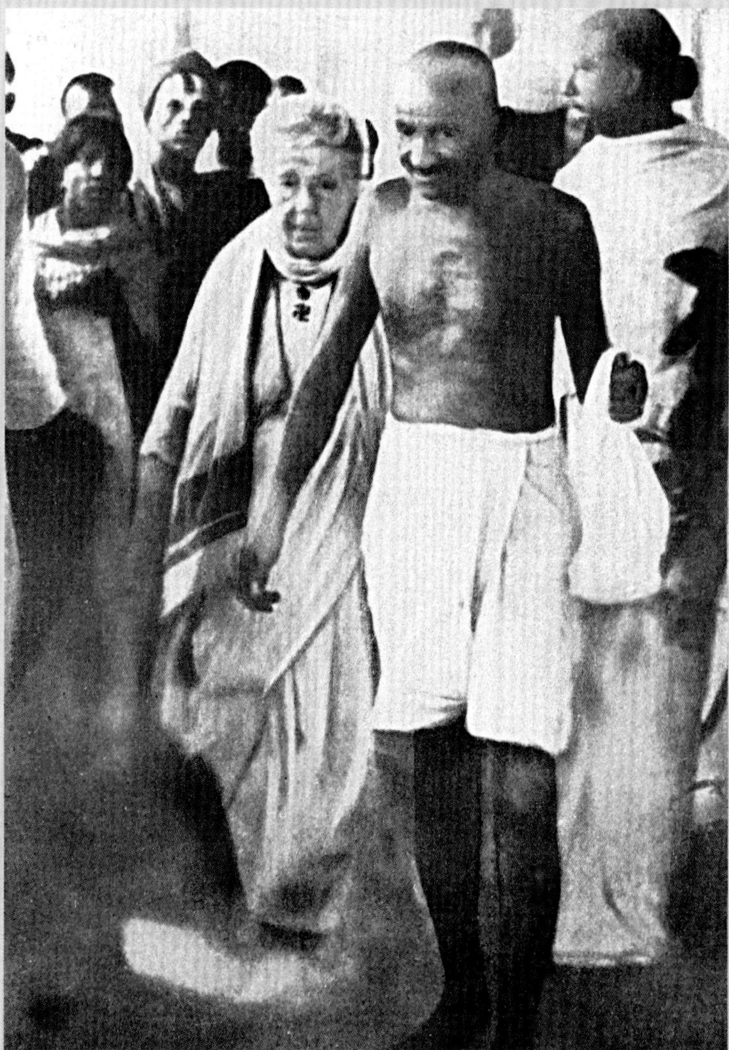

USA. To conciliate the moderates and avoid any political confrontation, Tilak started the Home Rule League asking, like the Irish Home Rulers, for administrative reforms and not for overthrow of the government. Annie Besant, an Irish ex-suffragette, an advocate of Free Thought, Fabianism and Theosophy came to India in 1893 to work for the Theosophical Society. She entered Indian politics in 1914 and founded the Home Rule League . She realised that for her movement to succeed, she had to get the support of the Indian National Congress, of both the Moderates and the Extremists. She launched a campaign through her two papers, *New India* and *Commonweal* and organised public meetings and conferences demanding that India be granted self-government on the lines of Britain's White colonies after the War. In 1917, the Government of Madras placed Mrs Besant and her associates B.P. Wadia and George Arundale under arrest. There was nation-wide protest and many 'Moderate' leaders like Madan Mohan Malaviya, Surendranath Banerjea and M.A. Jinnah joined the Home Rule League to show their support to Annie Besant. Tilak advocated the use of passive resistance if the government did not release her. At Gandhiji 's instance about a thousand signatures were collected of men who were prepared to defy the internment order and march to the place where Besant was interned. The new Secretary of State, Lord Montagu was much more sympathetic and conciliatory and Besant was released. She was elected President of the Indian National Congress in 1917.

The announcement of the Montagu-Chelmsford Reforms divided the ranks of the supporters of Home Rule and the movement gradually lost its strength. In any

Members of the Women's Indian Association
who met Montagu and Chelmsford

M.K. Gandhi during the Satyagraha struggle, South Africa, 1913

case, its popularity had been mainly among the urban, English educated intelligentsia. However, it had generated a widespread nationalist atmosphere and created a group of individuals who played an important role in the national movement of the succeeding years, when under the leadership of Gandhi, it became a mass movement.

SEEDS OF SATYAGRAHA AND CIVIL DISOBEDIENCE IN SOUTH AFRICA

It was in South Africa where Gandhi spent twenty years, and evolved a method of political protest which he called *satyagraha*, which literally means 'truth force' or 'the struggle for truth'. Gandhi described it as 'a force which is born of truth and love or non-violence'.[8] For him, it was the end of a quest for a moral equivalent of war. Satyagraha was not passive resistance, but active opposition to any form of injustice. Martin Luther King Jr read intensively into the Gandhian philosophy as a new and powerful weapon against injustice. But the opposition had to be non-violent. In his own words, 'Non-violence is the greatest force at the disposal of mankind. It is mightier than the mightiest weapon of destruction'.[9] King recognised Gandhi's legacy of non-violence for the effectiveness of his own campaigns for racial integration. He became Gandhi's greatest disciple by embracing *satyagraha* as a method of struggle for the emancipation of blacks in America.

The Transvaal government introduced the Asiatic Law Amendment Ordinance which required every Asian man, woman or child above the age of eight to register his or her name with the Registrar of Asiatics. Failure to do so was a criminal offence. In response to the Black Act, a public meeting was held in the Empire Theatre in Johannesburg in September 1906, attended by about 3000 Indians who took a vow to defy the law in a non-violent manner. While the pledge was taken in 1906, *satyagraha* was launched one year later after all attempts at persuading the government to drop the bill failed. Gandhi appeared in court and asked for the harshest penalty of six months imprisonment with hard labour for organising defiance of the Registration Act. The magistrate, however, awarded him two months simple imprisonment. He gladly went to prison to enjoy what he called the 'the free hospitality of His Majesty's hotel.' This was the first of his many imprisonments and the first non-violent challenge to the racist regime of South Africa.

The Cape Town Supreme Court ruled in 1913 that all marriages not performed according to Christian rites were illegal. Naturally, the Indians in South Africa were deeply agitated and *satyagraha* was launched both in Natal and Transvaal. This time women including Kasturba joined the struggle. They were arrested and imprisoned.

Before the Boer War (1899–1902), there had been no restriction on Indians migrating from one province to another. But the Natal government started feeling that the existence of 'free' Indians would undermine white hegemony and a £3 tax was imposed on all 'free' Indians to force them back to be indentured labour or return to India. Gandhi opposed this discriminatory law. The mine workers of Natal went on a strike and about 2000 of them started entering Transvaal without a permit. Gandhi decided to march on foot with them. The Great March began in October 1913.

Transvaal Women Association
STANDING LEFT TO RIGHT Mrs M. Tommy, Mrs K. Murugasa Pillay, Miss Baikum Murugasa Pillay, Mrs P.K. Naidoo
SITTING LEFT TO RIGHT Mrs Perumal Naidoo, Mrs Chinsamy Pillay, Mrs Thambi Naidoo, Mrs N. Pillay, Mrs Bhawani Dayal

Gandhi was arrested thrice and released on bail, but finally he was prosecuted on the charge of inducing indentured labour to disobey the law and leave Natal without paying the tax.

Under pressure from London and Delhi, Gandhi was released. Negotiations began and the Indian Relief Act was passed whereby the major points, on which the *satyagraha*s had been launched, were conceded. The £3 tax was abolished, marriages performed according to non-Christian rites were legalised and a domicile certificate bearing the holder's thumb impression was accepted as sufficient evidence of the right to enter South Africa.

It was in South Africa that Gandhi developed his ideas of non-violence, practising them as a means of fighting racial discrimination. This was his first successful attempt to employ non-violent civil disobedience. It was supported by sympathetic Europeans, Africans and Chinese. He was able to mobilise Hindus, Muslims, Jews, Parsis and Christians, miners, plantation workers, women and traders in defying unjust laws, abandoning their homes, facing starvation and physical violence, and courting imprisonment without raising a finger against their opponents.

Gandhi and Kasturba in South Africa, 1913

Miss Thomas
Rendered valuable service during the strike of Newcastle, 1913

LEFT TO RIGHT

Millie Polak

A close English friend of Gandhi in South Africa, she was the founder of the Transvaal Women Association

Valliamma Moonsamy

Died after serving a term of imprisonment as a passive resistence in South Africa

Mrs Sivaprasad, Ms Minnatjee and Mrs Somar who went to jail in South Africa

Ms Valliamma Moonsamy, Mrs Mahabeer,
Mrs Veerasamy, Mrs V.S. Naidu, Mrs V.S. Pillay
and Mrs Moonsamy Mudali spent three months in Jail

Gandhi in Champaran, 1917

Gandhi's Return to India

Gandhi went to South Africa in 1893 as an unknown barrister. He returned to India in 1915 as a well known public figure and political organiser. With his political experience and success in mind, he now wanted to use his technique of *satyagraha* for India's freedom struggle. On arrival in Bombay by S.S. Arabia, he was allowed to disembark at Apollo Bunder which was a very special privilege. He was received by a number of prominent leaders including Gopal Krishna Gokhale, Sir Pherozeshah Mehta, Sir Cowasji Jehangir, B.G. Horniman, editor of *Bombay Chronicle*, and Muhammad Ali Jinnah. He was driven through the streets of Bombay where large crowds lined the roads showering petals and garlanding him. A number of receptions were organised where speeches were made praising his work in South Africa. At a grand reception held in Petit Hall, the palatial residence of Jehangir Petit, where the elite of Bombay—around 600 prominent citizens, both Indian and Europeans had assembled, Gandhi

Gopal Krishna Gokhale (1866–1915)
A 'moderate', presided over the Congress session in 1906. Founded the Servants of India Society. Gandhi called him his political guru

arrived dressed in a Kathiawari *angarkhan, dhoti* and turban, and Kasturba in a white *khadi* sari. Gandhi felt a complete rustic and was dazzled by the pomp and splendour. Sir Pheozeshah Mehta presided over the function and among those present were Sir Richard Lamb, Sir Dorabji Tata, M.A. Jinnah, and Sir Dinshaw Wacha.[10] He did not dare to speak in Gujarati. Gandhi was not an impressive orator and many, who had expected him to be a fiery orator, were disappointed by his speech.

A garden party was hosted by the Gurjar Sabha in honour of Gandhi and Kasturba at Mangaldas House, Girgaum. The meeting was presided over by Jinnah who was President of the *sabha*. It brought Gandhi and Jinnah together on the same platform. K.M. Munshi who presided over the function said that Gandhi embodied in him the spirit of self-sacrifice and honour.

Shortly after his arrival, Gandhi went to his birthplace, Porbundar, to meet his sister and other relatives. He took a train to Rajkot travelling third class. Gandhi went to Poona to meet Gokhale whom he regarded as his political mentor and guru. Gokhale advised him to go around India and understand the ground reality before joining active politics. From Poona, Gandhi went to Shantiniketan to meet Rabindranath Tagore who was away. While he was there, he got the news of Gokhale's death and rushed to Poona. But he returned to Shantiniketan and met the poet. Though Gandhi attended the annual sessions of the Indian National Congress at Lucknow and Calcutta, he was not an active participant and spent a year travelling around India trying to understand the people and their minds keeping away from politics as per Gokhale's advice.

Gandhi with Kasturba at Jetpur, Saurashtra, 1915

Gandhi with Kasturba— returned from South Africa to India, 1915

Public reception to Gandhi at Karachi, 1916

Gandhi, Kasturba, Yakub Hasan and G.A. Natesan at Madras, 1915

Gandhi and Kasturba with C.F. Andrews, Prof. Rudra and faculty members at St Stephen's College, Delhi, 1915

TESTING THE WATERS: EXPERIMENTING WITH LOCAL PROBLEMS

Champaran

A new era started in India's freedom struggle when Gandhi launched his first experiment with *satyagraha* in India in Champaran district of Bihar in April 1917 for redressing the suffering and grievances of the indigo cultivators.

Indigo was being cultivated in north Bihar for over a century. The plantations were owned largely by British planters who sold the indigo at a very high price in the markets of London and Europe making huge profits. The peasants were, however, paid a pittance and were forced to cultivate indigo under the *tinkathia* system. Twenty *kathias* were equal to one acre and peasants were forced to cultivate indigo on 3/20th of this. In addition to the regular tax, the *amlas* or Indian subordinates of the European planters exacted numerous illegal taxes or *abwabs* from the peasants who were forced to perform free duties for the planters.

From the beginning of the twentieth century, the *raiyats* of Champaran were time and again protesting against their oppression. But the administration supported the planters and these violent protests were crushed. Legal battles were fought but the peasants were too poor and could not afford to go to court.

Raj Kumar Shukla of Bettiah, who had himself suffered, decided to take up the cause of the indigo cultivators. He went to the Lucknow session of Congress 1916 and met Madan Mohan Malaviya and Lokmanya Tilak and urged

Champaran *satyagrahi*s
(seated) Dr Rajendra Prasad, Anugrah Narayan Sinha,
(standing) Ram Navami Prasad, Sambhusaran Verma

Janakdhari Prasad

Inhuman working conditions of the workers of indigo factory

FACING PAGE Raj Kumar Shukla, a peasant who brought Gandhiji to Champaran

them to take up the cause of the indigo cultivators, but they replied that the country's political freedom was their first priority. Shukla had heard about Gandhi's struggle in South Africa, so he met him and urged him to do something for the poor peasants of Champaran. Gandhi said that he could give no opinion unless he saw the condition with his own eyes. Shukla persistently pursued Gandhi all over the country till Gandhi ultimately agreed rather reluctantly, as he knew little about the area or the problem. He was in Calcutta and accompanied by Shukla, left for Champaran.

On his way to Champaran, Gandhi arrived in Patna with only a small bundle of bedding, some papers and a box of dry fruits. This was his first visit to the city. And he knew no one. Gandhi had assumed that Raj Kumar Shukla was an influential man, but in fact he was a very simple person. Shukla took him to the house of Rajendra Prasad, who was unfortunately in Puri and the servant paid no attention to the guests thinking that they were poor farmers of some low caste. Gandhi was not allowed to draw water from the well or use the toilet.

Mazharul Haq was a flourishing barrister in Patna whom Gandhi had known in London and had subsequently met at the Congress session in Bombay in 1915. Haq had extended an invitation to him to come and stay with him if he ever came to Patna. Gandhi sent him a note and Haq came immediately in his car and took him to his house. He suggested that Gandhi should first go to Muzaffarpur, the headquarters of the Planters' Association as well as of the Commissioner of Tirhut.

So from Patna, Gandhi went to Muzaffarpur where he met the Commissioner and told him that that he would visit Motihari and Bettiah to look into the grievances of the cultivators. The Commissioner said that this was unnecessary as the government was already looking into the matter. But Gandhi insisted on going. As soon as he entered Champaran, a notice under Section 144 of the Criminal Procedure Code was served on him by the Sub Divisional Officer of Motihari to quit the district. Gandhi had expected this and was not surprised.

Gandhi appeared in court before the Sub Divisional Magistrate and read a statement in which he said that he was taking the serious step of 'seemingly disobeying the order made under Section 144 of the Criminal Procedure Code … I have entered the country with the motive of rendering humanitarian and national services'. He said that he had come to help the *raiyats* who were saying that they were not treated fairly by the indigo planters. He fully understood the difficulty of the administration and as a law abiding citizen, his first instinct was to obey the order. But this would be violating his sense of duty to those for whom he had come. He could serve them only by remaining in their midst. He had decided 'to submit without protest to the penalty of disobedience...' He said, 'I have disregarded the order served upon me, not for want of respect for lawful authority, but in obedience to the higher law of our being—the voice of conscience.' Gandhi returned the Kaiser-i-Hind Medal given to him by the government for the services rendered in World War I.

The news of the summons spread like wild fire and Motihari witnessed scenes it had never seen before. Thousands thronged the court where Gandhi appeared and the house where he was staying. Gandhi writes in his *Autobiography*, 'They (i.e. the government officials) understood that I didn't want to go against them, but wanted to politely oppose their orders. Thus they were not scared of me ... But they also understood that their authority had been undermined. For a moment people had left behind their fear of punishment.'[11]

The court was adjourned. Gandhi writes, 'Just before the court was to announce the verdict, I got an order from the magistrate that the Viceroy had said that the case should be withdrawn, and then I got the Collector's letter saying that I could carry on whatever investigation I wanted.'[12] It is believed that the Lt Governor of Bengal, Sir Edward Gait played a role and the Rev. C.F. Andrews was also responsible in having the order withdrawn. The newspapers reported this at length and Champaran and Gandhi's investigation got a great deal of exposure.

Gandhi collected around him a group of individuals who became his lifelong followers. Among them were Rajendra Prasad, Anugrah Narayan Sinha, Ram Navami Prasad, Braj Kishore Prasad—all affluent lawyers who charged enormous fees. Gandhi told them that they would have to translate the documents in Kaithi or Urdu, as well as the evidence recorded in Bhojpuri into English as he did not understand these languages, but he could not pay them for this. They agreed. Mahadev Desai and Narhari Parikh, two young men from Gujarat and J.B. Kripalani, who was a professor in the Muzaffarnagar College, also joined. Gandhi and his band of followers worked from dawn to dusk and tirelessly collected evidence of thousands of ryots. The evidence of about 8000 peasants was recorded. As he did not want to hurt or irritate the planters, but to win them over by gentleness, he made it a point of writing to them and meeting them. He met the Planters' Association and placed the ryots' grievances before them. The voluminous evidence was summarised and submitted to the government. After a prolonged exchange of letters between government officials and Gandhi, and a long meeting between Gandhi and the Lt Governor of Bengal, Sir Edward Gait, an Enquiry Committee was appointed to go into the whole issue. Gandhi was nominated as one of its members. Armed with evidence collected from 8000 peasants, Gandhi could convince the Committee that the *tinkathia* system needed to be abolished and the peasants should be compensated for the illegal increase in their dues. As a compromise, the planters agreed to refund twenty five per cent of the money they had illegally taken from the peasants. Gandhi agreed.

Shri Dharnidhar, Shri Gorakh Prasad and Shri Braj Kishore Prasad
during Gandhi's mission in Champaran

Jivatram Bhagwandas Kripalani

Gandhi had come alone and as an unknown figure to Bihar. Six months later he was given a hero's farewell with 40,000 people seeing him off. Gandhi had succeeded in resolving the issues in a completely non-violent manner. Professor Gilbert Murray described this as 'a battle between a soul and a government…' It was very difficult, he said, for persons in power to deal with

> a man who cares nothing for sensual pleasure, nothing for riches, nothing for comfort, or praise or promotion, but is simply determined to do what he believes to be right. He is a dangerous and uncomfortable enemy because his body, which you can always conquer, gives you so little purchase upon the soul.[13]

Mill Workers' Strike, Ahmedabad

Plague broke out in Ahmedabd in July 1917 and many warpers fled to their villages. This put the functioning of the mills in jeopardy. The mill owners realised that the only way to prevent this exodus was to pay them higher wages as plague bonus which amounted to 75 per cent of the regular wages. The Muslim, Baniya and Brahmin warpers who lived in the city and did not flee because they had nowhere to go were denied the increase.

A warper's wage at that time was 12 *pies*. The warpers decided to ask for a 25 per cent increase. They needed moral support and some guidance and turned to Anasuya Sarabhai who was already conducting a school and other welfare work in the Amarpura *chawl*. Anasuya advised them to put down their demand in writing and give the mill owners 48 hours to respond. This was for the first time in the history of the labour movement in Ahmedabad that a regular demand was made and notice served on the mill owners for higher wages. If the mill owners did not respond, the workers threatened to go on strike and this notice bore the signature of Anasuya Sarabhai. As the 48-hours-notice-period passed and there was no response from the mill owners, the warpers went on strike.

The strike went on for two months. Ultimately, the mill owners gave in. The warpers had demanded an increase of 15 *pies*. The mill owners, to save face, agreed to 14½ *pies*. Anasuya got the warpers to agree and the strike was called off.

As the plague started subsiding by the beginning of 1918, the mill owners decided to stop the plague bonus. Even before the mill owners had taken a formal decision,

Ambalal Sarabhai and Anasuya Sarabhai

rumours spread among the workers that their plague bonus was going to be stopped. The warpers' strike had just ended and now the rest of the workers demanded an increase. They argued that the bonus should continue to compensate for the increased cost of living.

Anasuya had successfully led the warpers' strike. Now the weavers and others came to her. The workers regarded her as their leader and trusted her implicitly, but to lead another strike was a tremendous responsibility. Her brother, Ambalal Sarabhai was the president of the Mill Owners' Association and was furious with her for getting involved in all this.

It was in this situation that Anasuya wrote to Gandhi asking for his guidance and blessings. There were between 15,000 to 20,000 workers and if they all went on strike, the entire textile industry would close down putting some 50,000 men out of work. A weavers' strike could not be taken lightly.

Gandhi was in Bombay when Ambalal called on him and apprised him of the situation in Ahmedabad. He told Gandhi of the decision to end the plague bonus and asked for Gandhi's intervention. Gandhi returned to Motihari in connection with the Champarn Satyagraha. But he decided that the Ahmedabad situation was serious and that he must act.

The British government was interested in a settlement and the then Collector of Ahmedabad, Chatfield, wrote to Gandhi that the mill owners were planning a lockout and he was informed that they would only heed his advice.

Gandhi asked Anasuya to call a meeting of representatives of workers from various mills. About a hundred turned up. After considerable argument and discussion, Gandhi persuaded the workers to demand only 35 per cent wage increase instead of their demand of 50 per cent. The mill owners were informed of this decision. They responded by forming their own labour committee with Ambalal to guide it.

Gandhi laid down certain rules for himself and his followers. They would visit the workers' houses and make detailed inquiries regarding their lifestyle and advise and help them in their difficulties.

Gandhi met the mill owners, the mill workers and the Collector, Mr Chatfield and had long discussions with them. It was agreed that an arbitration board should be set up. Despite this, workers in a few mills struck work. Gandhi held that the workers should not have gone on strike after an arbitration board had been appointed. But the mill owners were obviously waiting for an excuse. They argued that since the workers had stopped work after the appointment of an arbitration board, the arbitration process stood cancelled. They further announced that they would dismiss all workers who were not willing to work for 20 percent increase in wages.

The breach of agreement was regarded by Gandhi as a serious matter and he advised the workers to go on strike. After a careful study of the profits of the industry, the production costs and the cost of living, Gandhi felt that the workers would be justified in demanding an increase in wages. In response to the strike, the owners declared a lock out.

The strike began on 22 February 1918. From then on, every afternoon, at 5 o' clock, huge mass meetings were held under a *babul* tree outside Shahpur Gate addressed by Gandhi. Anasuya would bring him in her American car, a 1915 model, Overland Roadster, over the only bridge across the Sabarmati, available then. A crowd of not less than 5000 and sometimes 10,000 would be waiting for him to speak. Leaflets signed by Anasuya but often written by Gandhi, appealing to the workers to remain peaceful, united and disciplined, insisting that no violence be used against employers or blacklegs, were distributed. Thousands of workers paraded the streets peacefully with banners proclaiming *ek tek* (keep the pledge).

Anasuyaben led the workers while her brother Ambalal Sarabhai was the leader of the mill owners. Gandhi did his best to keep brother and sister on good terms. He invited Ambalal for a meal to his *ashram* and with a chuckle made Anasuya serve him. But on the dispute, Ambalal remained firm.

The strike went on for three weeks and the resolve of the workers began to weaken. They started complaining that while Gandhi and Anasuyaben were travelling by car and eating good food, they were on the verge of starvation.[14] Next day when Gandhi sat under the babul tree, he saw 'a thousand disappointed faces rather than the five thousand or more, beaming with self-determination' of earlier days. Realising that the workers might capitulate, Gandhi quietly said, 'I cannot tolerate for a minute that you break your pledge. I shall not take any food nor use a car till you get a 35 per cent increase.'[15]

Anasuya and several workers said that they too would go on a fast. But Gandhi told them that fasting was his business not theirs. The workers decided to continue the strike. The mill owners could not ignore the fast of a national activist like Gandhi and a compromise was worked out. On the first day that the workers called off the strike, they would get a 35 per cent increase in their daily wage. They could thus claim that their demand had been vindicated. On the second day, they would get only 20 per cent increase as that would honour the employers. Principal Anandshankar Dhruva was appointed as arbitrator, but in the meantime the workers and the mill owners agreed to a 27.5 per cent increase.

The settlement was announced at a public meeting where thousands gathered to hear Gandhi. After his speech, Gandhi broke his fast. He, Anasuya and Ambalal were taken around Ahmedabad in a carriage.

In the evening the workers assembled in Ambalal's spacious house where sweets were distributed. In his speech Gandhi said,

> It appears to me that as the days pass by, not only Ahmedabad but also India will be proud of this 22 days' struggle, and India will come to believe that where a struggle can be conducted in this manner, we can hope for much. The struggle has been conducted without any hostility... I have known many such conflicts directly or indirectly but I have not seen a single struggle where there was so little animosity or bitterness exhibited in the fight...[16]

In the wake of the fast came the launching of the Ahmedabad Textile Labour Association, the Majoor Mahajan, Gujarat's first union. Shortly afterwards, Principal Dhruva awarded 35 per cent increase.[17]

Members of the Joint Board of representatives,
Textile Labour Association

Mahatma Gandhi, April 1944

Satyagraha, Non-Cooperation and Civil Disobedience in India

In the application of satyagraha, I discovered in the earliest stages that pursuit of truth did not admit of violence being inflicted on one's opponent but that he must be weaned from error by patience and compassion. ...the doctrine came to mean vindication of truth, not by infliction of suffering on the opponent, but on oneself.

—M.K. Gandhi[18]

KHEDA SATYAGRAHA

As soon as the Ahmedabad mill workers' strike was resolved, Gandhi became involved with problems faced by the peasants of Kheda, in Gujarat, who were in distress because their crops had failed due to excessive rains and they were in no position to pay the land revenue. Their

Sardar Vallabhbhai Patel with colleagues, Shri Jivanlal Diwan, Shri Indulal Yagnik, Shri Ganesh Mavlankar, Shri Mohanlal Pandya and others during Kheda Satyagraha

FACING PAGE
Ganesh Vasudev Mavalankar

appeals to the government for remission of land revenue were being ignored. When this was brought to Gandhi's notice, he ordered a survey to be made of the 600 affected villages. For the first time *ashram* workers and youngsters came together to conduct this survey. Gandhi asked them to complete their work within 15 days. They had to travel on foot from village to village and eat only peanuts and roasted gram. The survey confirmed that the crops were less than one-fourth of the normal yield and that they were entitled under the revenue code to a remission of the land revenue for the season.

Appeals and petitions having failed, Gandhi initiated a no-tax campaign and big and small farmers rallied under his leadership. He urged them to 'fight unto death against such a spirit of vindictiveness and tyranny' and show 'that it is impossible to govern men without their consent'. Vallabhbhai Patel, a young lawyer and native of Kheda, and other young men including Indulal Yagnik joined Gandhi in

Sardar Vallabhbhai Patel

Gandhiji in Kheda, 1918

touring the villages and urging the peasants to stand firm despite the authorities seizing their cattle and household goods and attaching the standing crops. The peasants were asked to take a solemn pledge that they would not pay; those who could afford to pay had to take a vow that they would not pay till the government agreed to suspend the collection of land revenue.

The struggle went on for three months. The peasants of Kheda who had suffered from plague, high prices and drought were beginning to weaken in their resolve when Gandhi learnt that the government had issued secret orders directing that revenue should be collected only from those cultivators who could afford it. It was difficult for the government to publicly declare this since it would be a loss of prestige, and since this was exactly what Gandhi had been asking for. Under these circumstances Gandhi decided to withdraw the movement. Gandhi later admitted that by this time the peasants were exhausted and he was looking for 'some graceful way of terminating the struggle'.

Champaran, Ahmedabad and Kheda demonstrated Gandhi's style and method of politics. These were local struggles where Gandhi took up a specific issue, made a careful study of the problem and successfully resolved it by non-violent means. He now had a better understanding of the strengths and weaknesses of the ordinary people. He also earned a national reputation and the respect of many political workers who were impressed by his identification with ordinary Indians and his taking up their causes. With this experience and prestige, he was now ready to move to the national arena.

ROWLATT SATYAGRAHA AND THE JALLIANWALA BAGH MASSACRE

In view of the growing revolutionary activity during the First World War, Lord Chelmsford, the Viceroy, appointed a committee to investigate into the nature and extent of such activities. The committee suggested the introduction of two bills in the Imperial Legislative Council and in March 1919, one Anarchical and Revolutionary Crimes Act was passed which was popularly known as the Rowlatt Act after the man who chaired the committee. It provided speedy trial of offences by Special Courts free to accept evidence not covered by the Evidence Act. Provincial governments were given powers to search and arrest a person without a warrant only on suspicion. It aimed at severely curtailing the civil liberties of Indians in the name of curbing terrorist violence.

As soon as the two bills were introduced on 6 February 1919, Gandhi called them 'unjust, subversive of the principles of liberty and destructive of the elementary rights of the individual.' Gandhi suggested that a *satyagraha* be launched and a Satyagraha Sabha was formed with Gandhi as President. In the first stage of the *satyagraha*, volunteers courted arrest by defying the law and in the second stage a nationwide struggle was launched. 6 April 1919 was chosen for the observance of a nationwide *hartal* (strike) accompanied by fasting and prayer. In addition, it was decided that civil disobedience would be offered against specific laws.

The movement that emerged was very different from what had been planned. Anti-Rowlatt agitation was

Way to Jallianwala Bagh

FROM THE TOP

Jallianwala Bagh Massacre, 13 April 1919

Police atrocity during marshal law

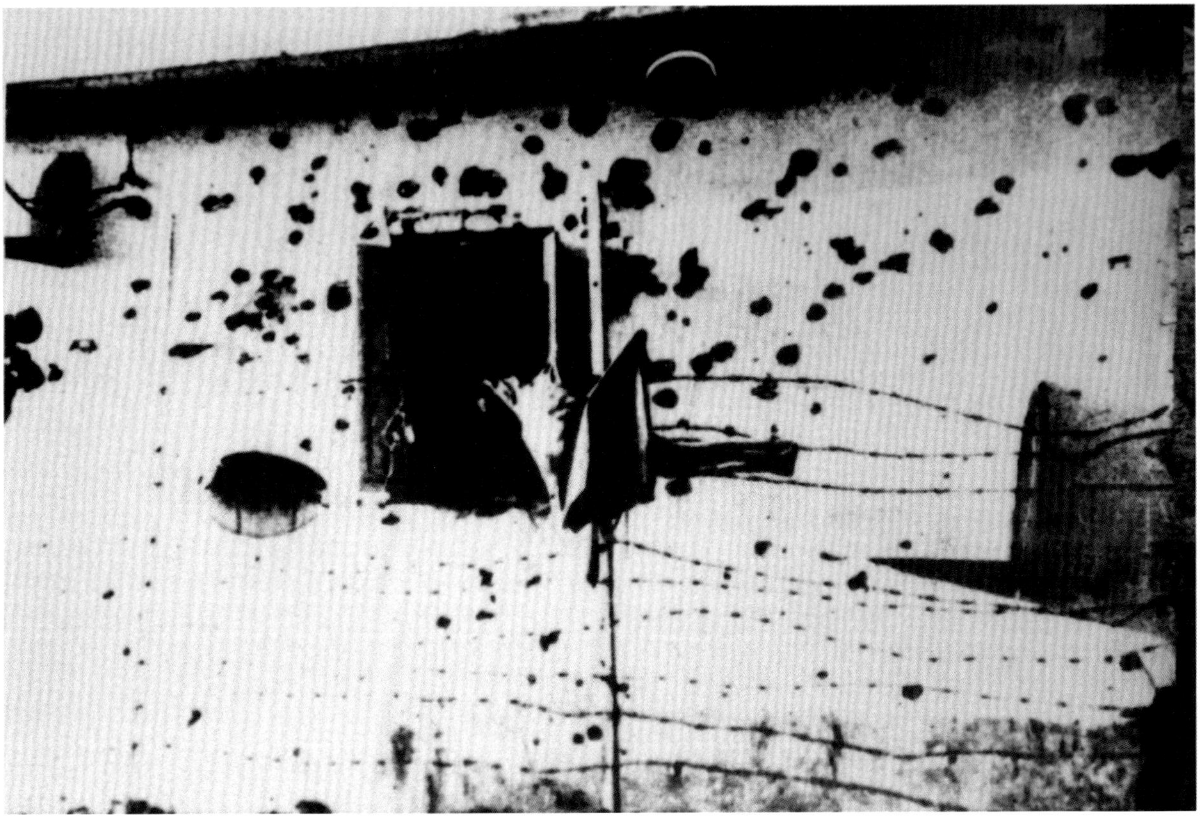

Bullet marks on the wall

particularly severe in Punjab which was suffering from after-effects of wartime repression, forcible recruitment and the influence of the revolutionaries. The situation in Lahore and Amrtisar became particularly dangerous for the government. Gandhi wanted to go to Punjab to defuse the tension but the government deported him to Bombay. He found that violence was spreading to Bombay and Ahmedabad and stayed on to pacify the people. The Punjab government ordered the arrest of two Congress leaders: Dr Satyapal and Dr Kitchlew. This led to an attack on the Town Hall in Lahore and the post office; telegraph wires were cut and Europeans, including women, were attacked. The army was called in and the city was handed over to General Dyer, who issued an order prohibiting public meetings and assemblies. On 13 April, Baishakhi day, a large crowd gathered in Jallianwala Bagh, Amritsar, to attend a public meeting. General Dyer, furious that his orders had been disobeyed, ordered his troops to fire upon an unarmed, peaceful crowd without warning, killing—according to government estimate—379 people, though the actual number was much higher according to other estimates.

Punjab was placed under martial law and the people of Amritsar were forced into indignities such as crawling on their bellies before Europeans. Faced by this atmosphere of violence, Gandhi withdrew the movement on 18 April. This did not imply that he had lost faith in non-violence and satyagraha. A year later he launched another nation-wide agitation on a much bigger scale.

NATIONWIDE AGITATION: NON-COOPERATION AND KHILAFAT MOVEMENTS

The Khilafat Movement was the result of the resentment of Indian Muslims over the defeat in World War I of the Ottoman Turkish empire along with its allies— Germany and Austria-Hungary. With rumours spreading about a harsh peace treaty to be imposed on the defeated Ottoman empire, the Khilafat Movement started gaining momentum in 1919–20. Its three central demands as articulated by Mohammad Ali were that the Turkish Sultan— the Khalifa— must retain control over the sacred Muslim places, must be left with sufficient territory to allow him to defend the Islamic faith, and the Jazirat-ul-Arab (Arabia, Syria, Iraq, Palestine) must remain under Muslim control. The movement had a moderate and a radical wing. The former was supported by Bombay businessmen, the latter by lower middle class journalists and *ulama* who had influence in small towns and villages of Uttar Pradesh, Bengal, Sind and Malabar. Gandhi initially played a mediating role between the two groups. He was also the link with the Hindu politicians as the Khilafat leaders were extremely eager for Hindu-Muslim unity for the success of their movement. With the publication of the harsh terms of the Treaty of Sevres (1920) with Turkey on 14 May 1920, followed by the Hunter Commission Majority Report on the Punjab disturbances, which Gandhi described as 'page after page of thinly disguised official whitewash', the tide turned in favour of the radicals.

The meeting of the Central Khilafat Committee (1– 3 June 1920) in Allahabad attended by a large number of Congress leaders saw the victory of the radicals who were backed by

Demonstration of protesters during
the Non-Cooperation Movement

Demonstration of protesters during the Non-Cooperation Movement

FACING PAGE **Lala Lajpat Rai (1905–1928)**
Known as 'Punjab Kesari'; a member of the Arya Samaj, he participated in the anti-Simon Commission protests

Gandhi. Its four fold programme of Non-Cooperation was announced-renunciation of titles, resignation from jobs held the civil service, police and army, and refusal to pay taxes.

At a special session of the Congress held in Calcutta in September 1920, a resolution was passed stating that 'there is no course left open for the people of India but to approve ...the policy of progressive non-violent non-cooperation. Gandhi urged the delegates to adopt a plan similar to the Khilafat Conference around the issues of 'Punjab wrong', the 'Khilafat wrong' and Swaraj, the last being rather vague. Full support initially came only from Gujarat and Bihar. Motilal Nehru was at first hesitant about the issue of boycott of council elections which were to be held in November 1920. C.R. Das and the Tilakites were bitterly opposed to it.

There was a dramatic conversion of the senior leaders such as Motilal, Lala Lajpat Rai and C.R. Das to Gandhi's programme in the next three months. The Calcutta Resolution was ratified unanimously at the Nagpur session in December 1920.

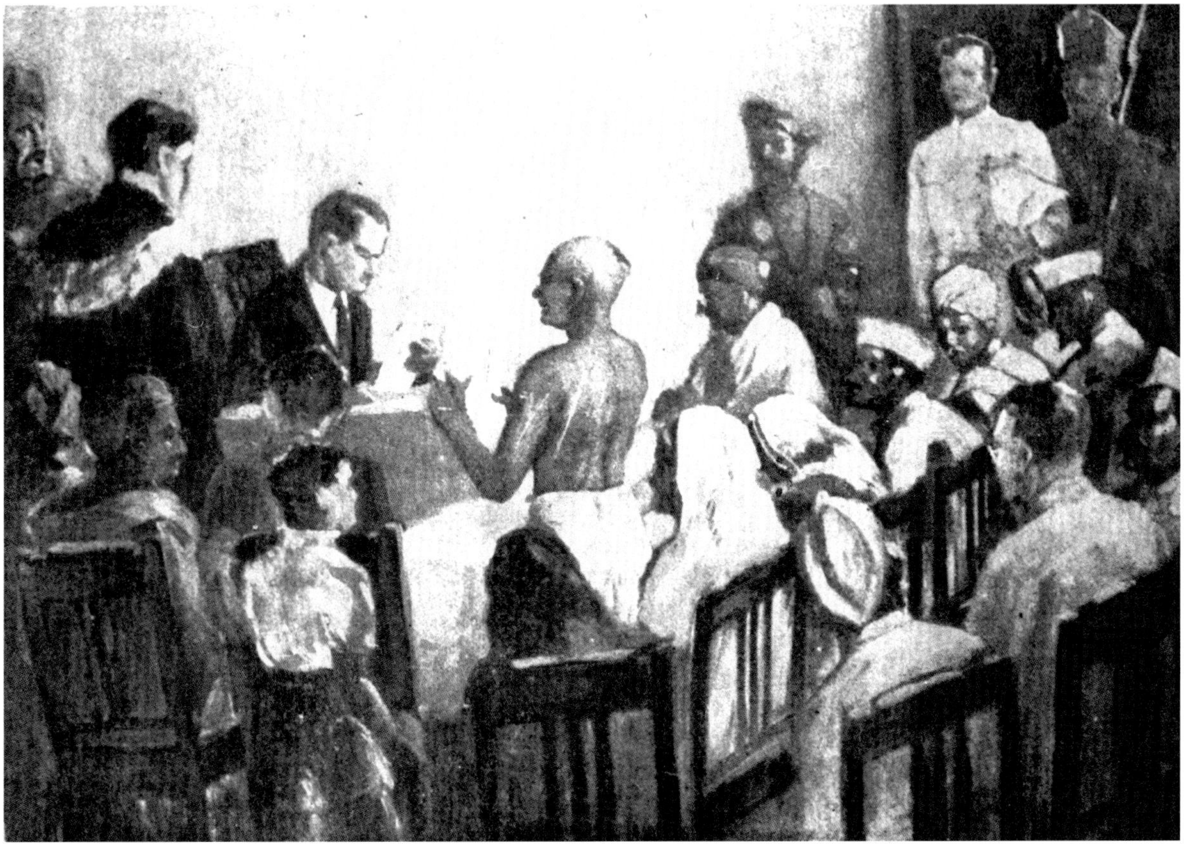

Appearing before the Court at Ahmedabad for sedition charges

Thus, the first all-India mass movement was launched under Gandhi's leadership. He described the movement as a state of peaceful rebellion and called for the defiance of every single state-made law.

The movement had a spectacular beginning. In the first few months, the central emphasis was on students leaving government schools and colleges. There were massive student strikes in Calcutta and Lahore. P.C. Bamford's confidential *History of the Non-Cooperation Movement* reveals that thousands of students left government colleges, but not many left primary schools. A number of national school and colleges were founded like the Jamia Millia Islamia in Aligarh, later shifted to Delhi, the Kashi Vidyapith at Banaras and the Gujarat Vidyapith in Ahmedabad. Numerous 'national' institutions were started in Bihar and Orissa, Assam, Bengal, Bombay and U.P. Many of these did not last long because degrees from these were not recognised for jobs and further education. But some survived. The educational boycott was particularly successful in Bengal. C.R. Das played an important role in promoting the movement and Subhas Bose became the Principal of National College in Calcutta. Punjab also responded to the education boycott call. Lajpat Rai played a leading role there.

The boycott of law courts was not that successful though lawyers of the eminence of C.R. Das, Motilal Nehru, C. Rajagopalachari, M.R. Jayakar, Vallabhbhai Patel, T. Prakasam and Asaf Ali gave up their lucrative legal practices and their example was an inspiration for many.

Perhaps the most successful part of the programme was the boycott of foreign cloth. Gandhi went round the country appealing, especially to women, to give up wearing imported clothes and practise *swadeshi*. Women responded enthusiastically to his call. Volunteers went from house to house collecting foreign clothes and bonfires were lit on street corners and *mohalla*s. Picketing of shops selling foreign cloth also became part of the boycott. 'The value of imports of foreign cloth fell from Rs. 102 crores in 1920–21 to Rs. 57 crores in 1921–22'.[19] Toddy shops were also picketed and government revenue showed considerable decline here also.

Congressmen and women were now asked to concentrate on collecting money for the Tilak Swaraj Fund, enroll members and popularise the *charkha*. The Tilak Swaraj Fund was oversubscribed; a vigorous membership drive was launched and though the target of a crore members could not be achieved, 50 lakh members were enrolled; *charkha*s were distributed widely and *khadi* became the uniform of Congressmen and women.[20] At a meeting when some students complained that *khadi* was too expensive, Gandhi replied that one should wear less clothes and from then on; he gave up his *dhoti* and *kurta* and started wearing a *langoti*[21], which he did for the rest of his life.

The Prince of Wales visited India in November 1921. A *hartal* was observed all over the country on the day he landed in Bombay. Gandhi addressed a mammoth meeting in the compound of the Elphinstone Mill in Bombay and lighted a huge bonfire of foreign cloth. Eurasians, Parsis and Jews came out to welcome the Prince. Crowds returning from Gandhi's meeting attacked them and full scale rioting broke out across the city. Shops, buildings, trams and cars were set on fire. Police firing took place and three days of

PUBLIC MEETING

AND

BONFIRE OF FOREIGN CLOTHES

Will take place at the Maidan near Elphinstone Mills

. . . Opp. Elphinstone Road Station . . .

On SUNDAY the 9th Inst. at 6-30 P. M.

When the Resolution of the Karachi Khilafat Conference and another Congratulating Ali Brothers and others will be passed.

Bonfire of foreign clothes

Protesters demonstrating the *charkha* to the masses

violence resulted in the death of 59 people. Gandhi was deeply disturbed and worried. He drove round the city trying to restore calm. He heard the rioters shouting 'Mahatma Gandhi *ki jai*'. He was horrified; 'never has the sound of those words grated so much on my years.' Gandhi was shocked and anguished at what his *hartal* call had turned into and said that he would go on a fast till peace was restored.

The Gandhian movement was, not surprisingly, strongest in Gujarat. Non-Cooperation remained relatively weak in Maharashtra where the followers of Tilak were not too enthusiastic about Gandhi. The movement penetrated the south. In Madras city there was a four-month-long strike at the British owned Buckingham and Karnatak Textile Mill which received the full support of the Non-Cooperation leaders.[22] Picketing of liquor shops was very successful in coastal Andhra and in Tamil Nadu under leaders like Rajagopalachari, Satyamurti and Kasturi Ranga Iyengar. Non-Cooperation was most successful in the Andhra delta region under leaders like Konda Venkatappayya, A. Kalessara Rao, T. Prakasam and Pattabhi Sitaramayya.

Most political leaders in Bengal accepted Non-Cooperation only after C.R. Das's conversion at the Nagpur Congress. Das, together with his three young lieutenants—Birendranath Sasmal in Midnapur, J.M. Sen Gupta in Chittagong, and Subhas Bose in Calcutta—succeeded in awakening the urban and rural masses.

One of the best organised rural movement was the anti-Union Board agitation in the Contai and Tamluk sub-divisions of Midnapur led by Birendranath Sasmal. The newly introduced Union Board brought about a heavy increase in local taxes and Sasmal was able to organise a very effective no-tax campaign among predominantly Mahishya tenants in November–December 1921 which forced the government to withdraw the new regulations. Students came out of government schools and colleges and national schools were established; foreign goods were boycotted and the use of *swadeshi* was propagated. Women of the area also played a significant role in resisting the payment of taxes. In the winter of 1921, peasants resisted Settlement operations in Pabna, Bogra and particularly in the Rampurhat sub-division of Birbhum.

Gandhi praised Bihar as 'a province in which the most solid work is being done in connection with Non-Cooperation. Its leaders understand the true spirit of non-violence'[23]. A large number of primary, high and middle level National schools were established. Depots were set up to distribute cotton and *charkha*s and khadi was produced on a large scale. Liquor boycott also made substantial progress.

The United Provinces became one of the strongest bases of the Congress during the Non-Cooperation Movement. It was during this time that some of the leading nationalists—Jawaharlal Nehru, Purushottamdas Tandon, Govind Vallabh Pant and Lal Bahadur Shastri came into prominence. Here also, national education institutions were set up, the most well known being the Kashi Vidyapith. The Gandhian impact on the intelligentsia was reflected in the novels of Premchand.

The unrest and defiance of authority generated by the Non-Cooperation Movement led to several local movements such as among the *kisans* in the Avadh area of U.P., the Moplah revolt in Kerala which assumed a communal colour, defiance of forest laws in Andhra, strike by plantation labour in Assam, and so on which were not non-violent.

On 5 February 1922, a Congress and Khilafat procession in Chauri Chaura in Gorakhpur district of U.P., provoked by the behavior of some policemen, attacked the police and when the latter hid inside the police station, the crowd set fire to it. Policemen who tried to escape were hacked to death. On hearing of this, Gandhi decided to withdraw the movement, the Congress Working Committee agreed and so, on 12 February 1922, the Non-Cooperation Movement came to an end.

In the Gandhian struggle, a mass movement was followed by a period of working within the constitutional and legal framework and carrying on constructive work among the masses till another mass movement was launched, what Professor Bipan Chandra described as Struggle-Truce-Struggle (S-T-S).[24] Madhavlal Shankarlal Pandya, an old participant from Borsad in Kheda district, Gujarat, put this strategy in his own colourful words: *lado* (fight), *jo mile so lo* (take what you can get), *bhogo* (utilise it), *phir lado* (fight again).[25]

BARDOLI SATYAGRAHA

Bardoli is a *taluka* in Surat district of Gujarat containing 137 villages. The bulk of the population in the 1920s were agriculturists. A number of Gandhiji's *satyagrahi*s in South Africa were from Bardoli. It was this that led Gandhi to approve Bardoli as an area in which to start his campaign of Civil Disobedience in 1921–22. The idea had to be dropped because of the sudden suspension of the Non-Cooperation Movement. However, considerable preparation had been

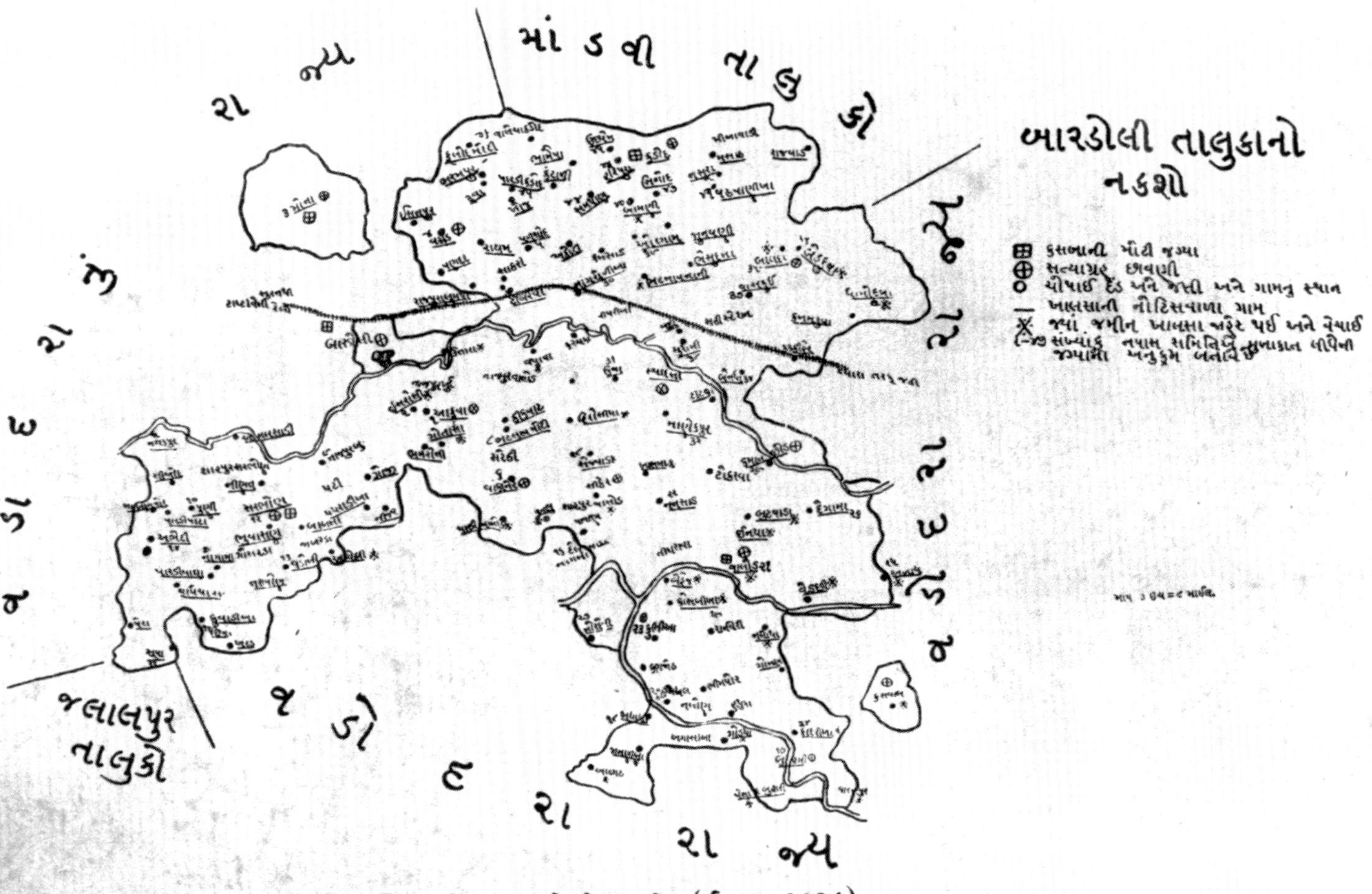

બારડોલી તાલુકા (ઈ. સ. ૧૯૨૮)

Map of Bardoli, 1928

made and the result was that the peasants had become politically conscious. Local leaders had worked hard to spread the message of non-cooperation. Almost all the Patels had given their letters of resignation to Gandhi to be delivered to the proper quarters at the right moment. National schools had been started in villages and the boycott of foreign cloth and use of *khadi* had spread widely. Social reform work among the untouchables and tribals, called *kaliparaj* (dark people) as distinguished from *ujaliparaj* (fair people) had also been taken up through several *ashram*s. Night schools were started to educate the *kaliparaj* and in 1927 a school for the education of *kaliparaj* children was set up in Bardoli town. Annual *kaliparaj* conferences were held and Gandhi presided over the conference in 1927 and initiated an enquiry into the condition of the *kaliparaj* whom he renamed *raniparaj*. The report of the enquiry was very critical of the *hali* system, under which they worked as hereditary labourers and were exploited by money lenders, and there was sexual exploitation of women by the upper castes. As a result of all this, the Congress had built a strong base among the lower castes in Bardoli. At the same time, the *ashram* workers had also worked among the upper castes.

The last land revenue settlement of the Bardoli *taluka* was made in 1896 and a revision was due in 1926. One Mr Jayakar was assigned to do the work. In his report he recommended an increase of 25 per cent over the existing rates but raised 23 villages from a lower group to a higher group, with the result that the total assessment of the *taluka* amounted to 30 per cent. The Congress leaders protested against this increase and set up the Bardoli

Gandhiji addressing a public meeting during
Bardoli Satyagragha, Surat, 1928

FACING PAGE Mohanlal Pandya

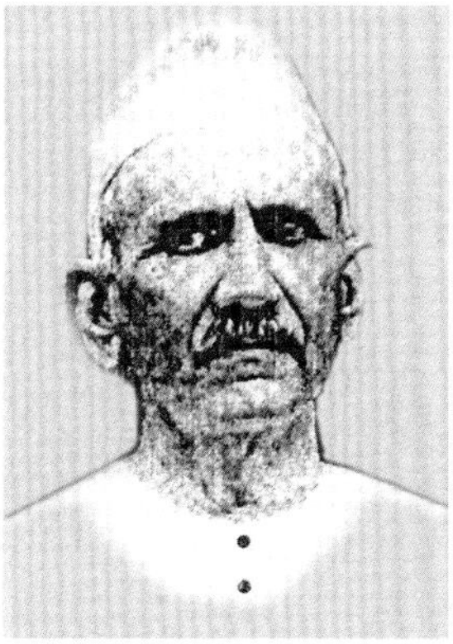

Inquiry Committee to examine the issue. The committee came to the conclusion that the increase was unjustified. A campaign was launched in the press mainly in *Young India* and *Navajivan*. Appeals were made to the government, but the government brushed aside the objections.

A deputation of peasants led by Mohanlal Pandya and Ravishankar Maharaj met Vallabhbhai Patel, who was then the President of the Gujarat Pradesh Congress Committee. They explained to him that the stiff increase in taxes was not only excessive but also arbitrarily fixed despite their protests and they were willing to offer *satyagraha*. Vallabhbhai, in his characteristic manner, asked for details and concrete facts. He explained to them the consequences and repeatedly urged them to be sure that the peasants were prepared for this. They presented him with a survey of sixty villages. Convinced by their data as well as their preparedness to face all dire consequences, he asked them to go and see Gandhiji, as a campaign like this could not be launched without his consent. Gandhiji grilled them and told them, 'Remember that you will have to keep the whole country with you, and the first condition is that your cause must be perfectly just... The people may be ready to fight. But do they know the implications of Satyagraha?' Vallabhbhai just arrived as this dialogue was going on. He said that he had studied the case and had no doubt that the cause was just. 'Well then there is nothing more to be considered,' said Gandhiji. 'Victory to Gujarat'.[26]

Vallabhbhai was ideally suited to lead this movement. He was an excellent organiser, an indefatigable campaigner and inspired the ordinary men and women of the region. Moreover, his family members were agriculturists who came from that area. He had a series of meetings with the peasants, the *ashram* workers and the constitutional leaders. He divided the *taluka* into thirteen workers' camps or *chhavni*s, each under an experienced leader. One hundred political workers, many of them students, formed the army of the movement. They were to organise meetings and meet the peasants individually and in groups. A publicity department was set up which brought out a daily *Bardoli Satyagraha Patrika*.

People were mobilised through propaganda, meetings, speeches, pamphlets and door to door persuasion. Women were not visible at first but they soon out-numbered men and singing patriotic songs thronged political gatherings and also organised their own meetings. Vallabhbhai made special appeals to them saying that in steadfastness of purpose, simplicity and purity, they were superior to men. Maniben Patel (daughter of Vallabhbahi), Mithuben Petit, Bhaktiba (wife of Darbar Gopaldas) and Sharda Mehta were some of the leaders. The women gave Vallabhbahi the title of 'Sardar'.

Abbas Tyabji and Imam Sahib Abdul Kazir Bavazir who had worked with Gandhi in South Africa, were put in charge of organising the Muslim peasants. They induced the peasants to sign the *satyagraha* pledge.

The men and women of Bardoli stood firm in their resolve not to yield to government threats. Their land was confiscated, their buffaloes, cows and implements seized.

Sardar Patel and his colleagues made a constant effort to carry the constitutionalists and moderate leaders as well as public opinion with them. Many members of the Bombay Legislative Assembly like K.M. Munshi and Lalji Naranji resigned their seats. By July 1928, even the Viceroy, Lord Irwin began to doubt the Bombay Government's position.

The face saving device was provided by the Legislative Council members from Surat who wrote a letter to the Governor assuring him that his pre-condition for an enquiry would be satisfied. The letter contained no reference to what the pre-condition was (though it was full payment of the enhanced rate) because an understanding had already been reached that that the full enhanced rent would not be paid. The Governor declared that he had secured 'an unconditional surrender'. But it was really the peasants of Bardoli who had won.

The enquiry conducted by a judicial officer, Broomfield, and a revenue officer, Maxwell, came to the conclusion that the increase had been unjustified and had reduced the enhancement. Gandhi said, 'the Bardoli struggle was not a struggle for the direct attainment of *swaraj*. ...That every such awakening, every such effort as that of Bardoli will bring *swaraj* nearer and may bring it nearer even than any direct effort is undoubtedly true.'[27]

A public meeting during Bardoli Satyagraha, Surat, 1928

SALT SATYAGRAHA/CIVIL DISOBEDIENCE

The Indian National Congress session in Lahore in 1929 adopted the goal of Purna Swaraj. On 26 January 1930, 'Independence Day' was observed throughout the country with a call to the people that 'it was a crime against God and man' to submit to the 'Satanic British rule.' The Congress authorised civil disobedience, i.e. defiance of government laws, but left the time and method of defiance wholly to Gandhi.

Gandhi believed that in *satyagraha*, your opponent must not be taken by surprise. He, therefore, sent a letter to Lord Irwin on 31 January, which was kind of an ultimatum consisting of a list of demands which included total prohibition, reduction of the rupee-pound ratio to 1 shilling 4 pence, reduction of land revenue by at least 50 per cent, abolition of the salt tax, etc. If the Viceroy accepted these demands, there would be no civil disobedience, then the Congress would willingly participate in the Round Table Conference in London. His letter was ignored.

Gandhi again wrote to the Viceroy on 2 March 1930, addressing him as 'Dear Friend'. He said:

> Before embarking on Civil Disobedience and taking the risk I have dreaded to take all these years, I would fain approach you to find a way out. My personal faith is absolutely clear, I cannot intentionally hurt anything that lives, much less fellow human beings, even though they may do the greatest wrong to me and mine. Whilst, therefore, I hold British rule to be a curse, I do not intend harm to a single Englishman

> or to any legitimate interest he may have in India. …I have the privilege of claiming many Englishmen as dearest friends, indeed much that I have learnt of the evil of British rule is due to the writings of frank and courageous Englishmen who have not hesitated to tell the unpalatable truth about the rule.[28]

Gandhi then went on to elaborate on why he regarded British rule as a curse—it had impoverished millions by maintaining a 'ruinously expensive military and civil administration which the country can never afford; it had reduced Indians to political serfdom; it had sapped the foundations of our culture … it has degraded us spiritually.'[29]

He said that all other avenues having failed, there seemed no other option except civil disobedience. He informed the Viceroy of his plan of action which was to disregard the salt law. Salt tax was five *annas* a year, which, said Gandhi, was equal to three days' earnings of a poor Indian and hence he considered it the most iniquitous of levies.

> I repudiate this law and regard it as my sacred duty to break the mournful monotony of compulsory peace that is choking the heart of the nation… it is, I know open to you to frustrate my design by arresting me. I hope that there will be thousands ready, in a disciplined manner, to take up the work after me…[30]

Lord Irwin didn't deign to reply. Instead, Gandhi got a curt reply from his Private Secretary that the Viceroy regretted that Gandhi was contemplating 'a course of action which is bound to involve violation of the law and danger to public peace'. Gandhi said that, 'I asked for bread and I have received stone instead.' He considered this rebuff as the final justification for battle.

Gandhi did not send the letter by post. Instead he chose Reginald Reynolds, a young Englishman who was staying at the *ashram* to deliver it in person. Gandhi used Reynolds to send a message to the world that it was not just Indians who were involved in a peaceful struggle against the British, but even some Englishmen supported the Indian cause.

The plan of action was brilliantly conceived. Gandhi declared that he would launch a civil disobedience movement and the weapon he chose was salt. He announced his intention of launching the *satyagraha* by breaking the salt law by marching from Sabarmati Ashram to Dandi, a sparsely populated village on the sea coast of Gujarat, about 200 miles from Ahmedabad. In retrospect, breaking the salt law seems an obvious choice. But at the time many thought it was a ridiculous idea. Even Congress leaders like Motilal Nehru doubted its efficacy. How was it going to lead to total independence? Indulal Yagnik, a Gujarat politician, who had worked closely with Gandhi in the Non-Cooperation Movement and in the Bardoli Satyagraha asked, 'Wouldn't the Salt Campaign fail to arouse the enthusiasm of the youth of the nation? Wouldn't they all see through the farce of wielding the sledgehammer of Satyagraha to kill the fly of the Salt Act?'[31]

Alternative suggestions were made: burning of foreign cloth on a mass scale, non-payment of land tax, forming a parallel government, a mass march to Delhi and so on. But Gandhi was firm. His mind was made up.

Walking was a habit which Gandhi had encouraged years earlier in South Africa. In his *ashram* called Tolstoy Farm, one of the rules made it compulsory for the inmates to use no transport when travelling to the nearest city. So what if Johannesburg was thirty miles away!

On 12 March at 6:30 am, Gandhi began his historic march to Dandi. The first batch of *satyagrahi*s numbered 79. Almost all of them were inmates of Sabarmati Ashram. They included men from all regions and religions including four untouchables. There were teachers, khadi students, and men in charge of various departments of the *ashram*. When the list prepared by Mahadev Desai was announced in the newspapers, Abbas Tyabji saw the name Abbbas and assumed that it was his, but wondered why he had not been contacted as only two days were left for the march. Tyabji rushed to the *ashram* only to be informed that the Abbas in the list referred to the 21 year old Abbas Varteji, a carding and weaving expert in Sabarmati Ashram who was a teacher in the *khadi* technical school. Gandhi made amends by asking Tyabji to go in a car and receive the marchers at designated halts. He gave him a real honour by designating him as his replacement when he was arrested.

As Gandhi marched to Dandi, men and women were everywhere on the way to greet him and hear him speak. In his speeches Gandhi exhorted women not to carry *chattie*s of toddy, to picket shops selling foreign cloth and liquor, to wear *khadi* and spin on the *charkha*. To popularise boycott of foreign cloth, a Videshi Kapad Bahishkar Samiti was formed in Ahmedabad. It organised daily processions in which women wearing saffron saris held meetings and issued cyclostyled sheets which were distributed

Gandhiji addressing the masses on the eve of Salt March
at Sabarmati riverbank, March 1930

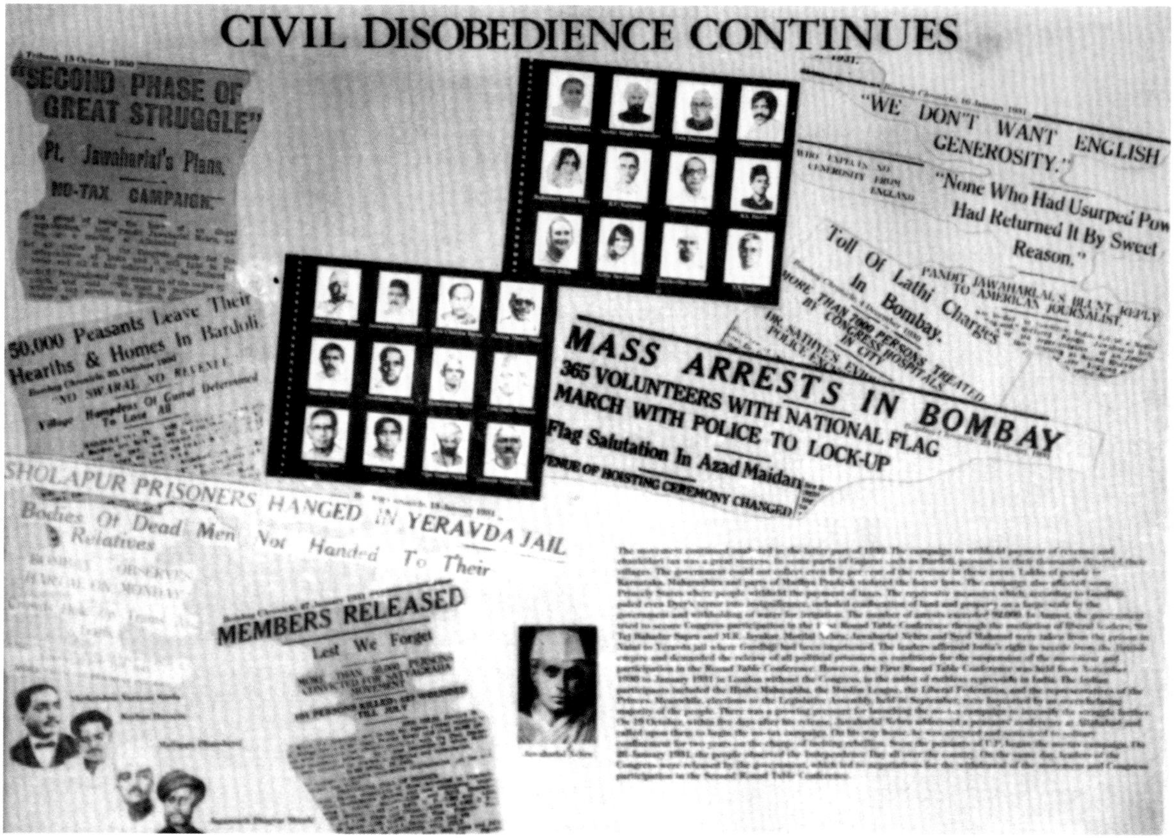

Headlines of the newspapers during the Civil Disobedience Movement

Gandhi (with stick), Sarojini Naidu, Abbas Tyabji
and the marchers at Dandi, 7 April 1930

Sketch of bonfire of foreign cloth

throughout the city.[32] They collected foreign cloth and lit bonfires with them. Volunteers went from door to door to collect signatures for the pledge of *swadeshi*. Trucks and carts carrying foreign liquor and cloth were stopped. Sale of contraband salt was taking place all over Gujarat.

The women of Sabarmati Ashram suggested that he should take at least four or five of them along with him; Gandhi said that just as it would be cowardice for Hindus to keep cows in front of them while going to war, similarly it would be cowardly to keep women with them on this march. But women refused to be restrained in this manner. The division of sexes in a non-violent movement seemed to women unnatural and contrary to the awakened consciousness of modern Indian womanhood. They felt that no marches, no demonstrations should take place without them. Khurshedben Naoroji, grand-daughter of Dadabhai Naoroji, wrote an angry letter asking Gandhi why he was preventing women from breaking the salt law. Margaret Cousins wrote an article in *Stree Dharma*, the journal of the Women's Indian Association, protesting against women's exclusion. 'In these critical stirring days of India's destiny, there should be no watertight compartments of service. Women asked that no conferences, congresses or commissions should be held without the presence of women. Similarly, women must ask that no marches, no imprisonments, no demonstrations organised for the welfare of India should prohibit women from a share in them.'[33] Durgabai Deshmukh was also against the idea of excluding women from the march. In her letter of protest to Gandhi, she wrote, 'we women should be allowed to join.'[34] Kamaladevi Chattopadhyaya was also deeply disappointed.

Mrs Amina A. Tyabji, Kamaladevi Chattopadhyaya
and Kasturba during Salt Satyagraha, 1930

Dadabhai Naoroji (1825–1917)
'Grand Old Man of India' was a founder member of the INC and was elected its President thrice

She rushed to Jambusar where Gandhi was scheduled to halt on his way to Dandi. She argued with him, and after some initial resistance, because of Kamaladevi's insistence, Gandhi finally agreed and gave her a slip of paper in which he wrote, 'All may regard this as the word from me that all are free and those who are ready are expected to start Civil Disobedience regarding the Salt Law from April 6th.'[35]

The route and the final destination had to be carefully planned. The leadership was provided by Vallabhbhai. Wherever Gandhi and his fellow marchers stopped, and Gandhi gave a speech, the audience needed to be large and enthusiastic. In order for this to happen, the route had to be planned in such a manner that it traversed areas where the support for Gandhi was the strongest. Between Ahmedabad and the coast, two areas were identified: Kheda district and Bardoli.

A week before the march began, thousands of people daily attended the prayer meetings at Sabarmati Ashram. On the evening of 11 March, when Gandhi held his last prayer meeting before setting off on the march, there was a record crowd of about ten thousand.

At 6:30 am on 12 March, the historic march to Dandi was to start. From early morning people were singing '*vaishnava jana to tena kahiye*'. As Gandhi marched to Dandi, he was greeted by thousands of men and women on the way. The roads was strewn with flowers and leaves, and villages and towns decorated with flags and banners. Everywhere crowds were shouting 'Mahatma Gandhi *ki jai*.' The news of his progress was widely reported in the press and by the time Gandhi and his party reached Dandi, the whole nation had been aroused. On 6 April 1930, by picking up a handful of

With salt *satyagrahis* Gandhi on the way to Dandi, Gujarat, March 1930

Gandhi addressing *satyagrahis* during Salt Satyagraha, March 1930

FACING PAGE Gandhi in a mass meeting during Dandi March, Gujarat, March 1930

Wounded *satyagrahi* being carried on a stretcher during the Salt Satyagraha, May 1930

FACING PAGE Sarojini Naidu receiving Gandhiji on the eve of Salt Satyagraha with Pandit Khare on right of Sarojini Naidu and Mithubehn Petit behind Gandhiji, 5 April 1930

salt, Gandhi inaugurated the Civil Disobedience Movement which unleashed country wide mass participation.

In Tamil Nadu, Rajagopalachari led a march from Trichinapoli to Vedaranniyam on the Tanjore coast. By the time he was arrested, he had prepared enough volunteers to carry on the *satyagraha*. In Malabar, K. Kelappan, hero of the Vaikom *satyagraha*, took the lead in breaking the salt law. In Andhra, military style camps were set up in different districts to serve as offices for conducting the *satyagraha*. A group of *satyagrahi*s walked from Sylhet in Assam to Noakhali on the Bengal coast to break the salt law. There were mass demonstrations in the North West Frontier Province led by Khan Abdul Gaffar Khan.

Bombay was agog with excitement. Three centres were set up in the city. The first was in the suburbs of Vile Parle where many Gujarati and Marwari families resided. Gandhi's close associate Jamnalal Bajaj set up the camp here, which included Kishorilal Mashruwala and Swami Anand. At the Congress House in Girgaum, a middle class Maharashtrian area, K.F. Nariman, Yusuf Meherally and other leaders of the B.P.C.C, were involved. In Parel and Matunga, working class localities, railway workers were mobilised.[36]

Gandhi nominated Jamnalal Bajaj as the first 'dictator'. On 6 April, Bajaj unfurled the national flag at a gathering in Vile Parle. After that, the *satyagrahi*s went to a saltwater pool and prepared salt.

From then on, celebrations started all over the city. Under the auspice of the B.P.C.C., a procession of about 2000 persons started from Congress House and marched through the city.

The front line unit to formally break the salt law consisted of 75 men and 2 women. As the procession marched towards Chowpatty, people from balconies and roof tops showered rose petals until the road became a carpet of flowers. Cries of '*nimak kaida toda hai, inquilaqb zindabad*' and 'Mahatma Gandhi *ki jai*' resounded the air. All over the city processions and meetings were held. Thousands gathered on Chowpatty to boil sea water and make salt. Packets of salt were sold by men and women volunteers. The *satyagrahi*s picketed shops selling foreign cloth and liquor. Police repression failed to suppress the enthusiasm of the people. 'Bombay's response to the Salt Satyagraha created history.'[37]

The Parsis, though a small community, participated in the Salt Satyagraha. Under the auspices of the Parsi Rajkiya Sabha, a public meeting was held on 21 May 1930 to congratulate the Parsi *satyagrahi*s who had been arrested. Resolutions were passed asking people to boycott foreign

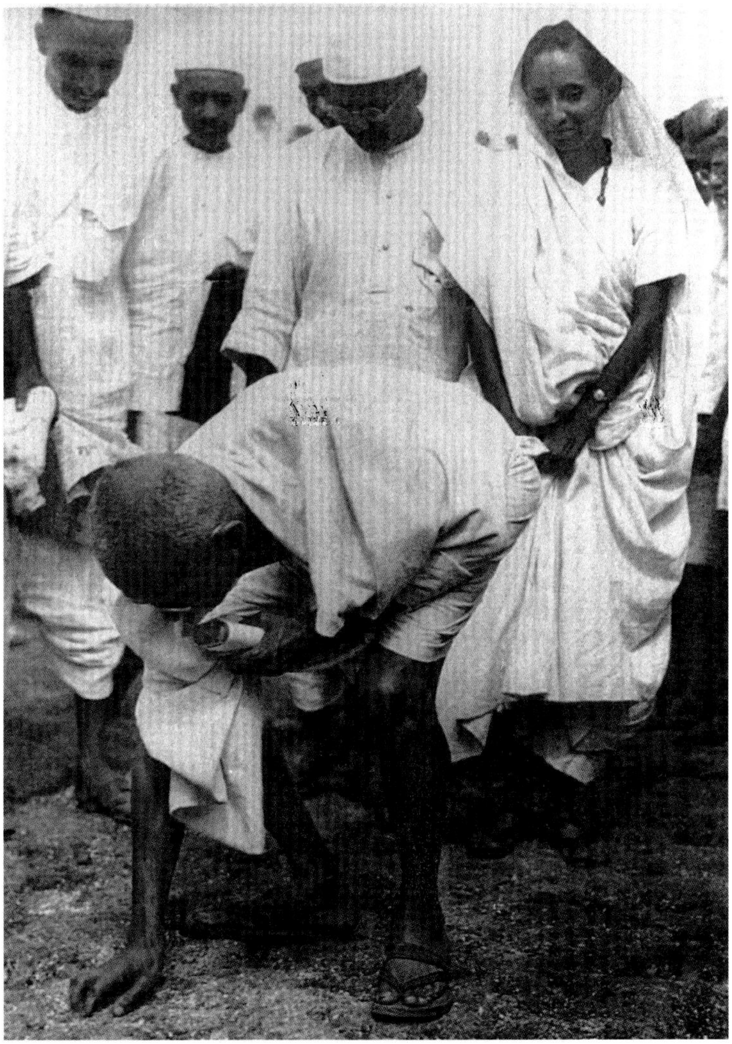

Breaking the salt law

The Salt Satygraha participants

Satyagrahis making human chain during Salt Satyagraha, May 1930

cloth and participate in the movement. A meeting of Parsis was held in Sir C.J. Hall on 12 June 1930, where the hall was overflowing and in the audience were many women. Perin Captain, who was to preside, was prevented from coming by the police blockade. A Parsi priest who spoke said that Parsis must join the struggle to prove that soul force was more powerful than bayonets and machine guns.[38]

A succession of salt raids on the Wadala salt depot was an important phase of the Salt Satyagraha in Bombay. Kamaladevi and many others were arrested. Hundreds of volunteers rushed towards the salt pans and despite police resistance, removed salt. They got arrested every day. This drama continued from 22 May 1930 and the biggest raid was on 1 June when nearly 15,000 volunteers participated. Successive batches marched towards the Port Trust level crossing where the police cordon stopped them. 'Soon the raiders, including women and children, broke through the cordon, splashed through slime and mud and ran over the pans.'[39] Police treatment of the raiders caused considerable indignation and protest, especially since a large number of women took part.

In Bengal, in the sea side districts of Midnapur, Khulna and Chittagong, thousands joined the movement and courted arrest. On 13 April 1930, the Jallianwala Day was celebrated by a huge procession which ended in Cornwallis Square where a meeting was held and contraband salt was sold.

Midnapur was once again active and the salt law was continually broken. All the leaders were arrested and police repression continued. Despite police *lathi* charge and beating people with boots and cane people did not lose their courage.

During the raid on Wadala Salt Depot in Mumbai, the police arrested the *satyagrahis*, 3 June 1930

Encirlement of Mumbai Merchants by the police at Boribundar (now Chhatrapati Shivaji Terminal) during Salt Satyagraha, 23 May 1930

Delhi was equally involved and one of the important leaders was Satyavati, the granddaughter of Swami Shradhhanand. The effectiveness of the picketing of foreign cloth was considerable and the Delhi Satyagraha Report of 1930 noted: 'On the whole we can safely say that not a yard of foreign cloth is being openly sold in Delhi...'[40]

The typical scenario in the cities of United Provinces was volunteers taking out processions with a hand cart with salt making paraphernalia on it. It would stop at street corners and salt would be made on the spot. The salt was then packed and sold at the rate of one *anna* per packet. The packets were sold instantaneously; such was the enthusiasm of the people.[41] Volunteers stood at street corners crying out 'We have broken the Salt Law and are free. Who will buy the salt of freedom?'

The movement spread all the way from the Tamil Nadu, Andhra Pradesh and Karnataka to the North West Frontier Province and from Assam to Gujarat. The government had hoped that that the enthusiasm would soon subside and Gandhi's strategy would fail. When this did not happen, the Viceroy was 'puzzled and perplexed' and finally ordered Gandhi's arrest. This led to a massive wave of protest all over the country from various sections of society, including merchants, shopkeepers, textile and railway workers, peasants, students and women. Going to jail was no longer a stigma but an honour. Aruna Asaf Ali remarked that for women it became almost like going to a temple! Peaceful demonstrations and *hartals* became a daily occurrence.

Faced with this, the Viceroy suggested a round-table conference as a conciliatory measure and expressed his willingness to discuss the goal of dominion status. The

The movement covered by the leading newspapers

British prime minister expressed the hope that the Congress would participate in it. Gandhi was released unconditionally on 25 January 1931. After prolonged deliberations, the Congress Working Committee authorised Gandhi to initiate discussions with the Viceroy that resulted in the Gandhi Irwin Pact on 5 March 1931.

India did not become independent till seventeen years later and so, in a way, Dandi March did not succeed in its objective. But the March and the Civil Disobedience Movement which followed, achieved much else. It gave a sense of empowerment to the participants. Gandhi had from the beginning asked people to be fearless. As Jawaharlal Nehru wrote:

> the dominant impulse in India under British rule was that of fear—pervasive, oppressing, strangling fear; fear of the army, the police, the widespread secret service ; fear of the official class; fear of laws meant to suppress and of prison; fear of the landlord's agent; fear of the moneylender; fear of unemployment and starvation, which were always on the threshold. It was against this all-pervading fear that Gandhi's quiet and determined voice was raised: Be not afraid.[42]

Gandhi said that once the *satyagrahi*'s mind is rid of fear, he will never agree to be another's slave. Swaraj was a process of freeing oneself. He had from the beginning emphasised the importance of being fearless. The Salt Satyagraha and the Civil Disobedience Movement were on a much a larger scale than the previous movements and involved many more people.

The Dandi March changed the way at least a section of the British public and the way the world viewed India. Web Miller, a correspondent for the United Press of America, became increasingly sympathetic to the national cause and influenced public opinion back home. Describing the Dharasana salt raid, he wrote:

> In complete silence, the Gandhi supporters halted a hundred yards from the stockade. The officers ordered the marchers to retreat. They continued to advance…. Suddenly, at a word of command scores of native policemen rushed upon the advancing marchers and rained blows on their heads with their steel-shod *lathis*. Not one of the members even raised an arm to ward off the blows. They fell like ninepins. From where I stood, I heard the sickening whack of clubs on unprotected skulls…Those struck down fell sprawling, unconscious or writhing with fractured skulls or broken shoulders. The survivors without breaking rank, silently and doggedly marched on till struck down.[43]

Miller noted that the police continued savagely kicking the men in the abdomen and testicles. But group after group of *satyagrahi*s continued to march. 'In 18 years of reporting in 22 countries…I have never witnessed such harrowing scenes', Miller wrote. His report appeared in newspapers round the world and Dharasana falsified Britain's claim that it was performing a 'civilising mission' in India.[44]

Police *lathi* charge on unarmed men and women undermined the notion of the benevolence of British rule. The process of undermining and creating an intellectual framework for it had already been started by Dadabhai Naoroji in his theory of drain of wealth in his book *Poverty and Un-British Rule in India*, where he developed a critique of the underdevelopment of India under colonial rule.

Another important message of the Salt Satyagraha was inclusion. Gandhi tried to involve Hindus, Muslims, Parsis, Untouchables, the poor villagers and the rich businessmen, the educated and the illiterate. As far as women were concerned, Dandi March was a revolution. Unarmed women faced *lathi* charge and police blows. Some 17,000 women were arrested during 1930–31. 'The veil of centuries was torn asunder. Women young and old, rich and poor came tumbling out in their hundreds and thousands, shaking off the traditional shackles that had held them so long'—wrote Kamaladevi.[45] Months after the Salt March when Gandhi met Lord Irwin, he took out a small packet of salt. 'I will put a little of this salt into my cup of tea', Gandhi said with a mischievous smile, 'to remind us of the Boston Tea party'. Lord Irwin laughed with him.[46]

Huge crowd waiting outside the Maidan, Kolkata

The Final Call—
Quit India Movement

The Second World War in Europe began in 1939. Gandhi was of the view that India should not participate in the war. However, he was ready to consider helping in the war effort if the government made a firm commitment that independence would be granted to India. As the government was not prepared to do so, he launched his individual *satyagraha*. The government had framed a Revolutionary Movements Ordinance which was to be promulgated if the Congress launched a movement. Gandhi, therefore, announced a very low key limited campaign in which only individuals who were specially selected would be allowed to join. The type of *satyagraha* they were to offer was more symbolic than real. They would give notice of their intention to deliver a speech against the war which was prepared by Gandhi and the speakers had to strictly adhere to it. Gandhi declared that this movement was merely to assert the right to freedom of speech. The campaign was inaugurated by Vinoba Bhave on 17 October 1940.

By 1942, Hitler had occupied most of Europe; he was constantly bombing Britain; and there was fear that his army would cross the English Channel. German troops were advancing towards the Soviet Union. On the Pacific front, the Japanese had captured Hong Kong, Malaysia and Singapore and the British had started withdrawing from Burma. Japanese invasion of India seemed imminent.

After the fall of Rangoon to the Japanese, under pressure from the United States, the British Government sent Sir Stafford Cripps, a member of the British Cabinet, to find out a future solution for India in consultation with Indian leaders. Cripps proposed the granting of Dominion Status, formation of a constitution, making a body consisting of elected representatives from the British provinces and Princely States immediately after the war, implementation of the constitution so made, with two conditions:

> (1) Provinces of British India if not prepared to accept the constitution would retain their present position and with such non acceding provinces, British Government might agree upon a new constitution or decline to do so.
> (2) Every Princely State would be free to adhere to the Constitution or decline to do so. Finally, an Executive Council would be set up consisting of the principal sections of the Indian people, but Britain would retain the control of defence as part of their war effort. Both the Congress and the Muslim League rejected the Cripps Offer.

In conversation with Sir Stafford Cripps in Delhi,
27 March 1942

The peoples' discontent was growing because of rising prices and wartime shortages. Gandhi came to believe that 'the presence of the British in India is an invitation to Japan to invade India and their withdrawal removes the bait.'

In this situation, Gandhi appealed to the British government to withdraw and leave India to her fate. 'For Heaven's sake leave India alone. Let us breathe the air of freedom.' This came to be known as the 'Quit India' resolution.

The Working Committee of the Indian National Congress met in Wardha on 14 July 1942 and passed a long resolution stating that 'British rule in India must end immediately.' It stressed India's need to feel 'the glow of freedom'. The All India Congress Committee, which met in Bombay on 7 and 8 August 1942, endorsed this resolution in substantially the same language. It resolved

> to sanction, for the vindication of India's inalienable right to freedom and independence, the starting of a mass struggle on non-violent lines on the widest possible scale so that the country might utilise all the non-violent strength it had gathered during the last twenty-two years of peaceful struggle. Such a peaceful struggle would be under the inevitable leadership of Mahatma Gandhi.[47]

The All India Congress Committee (AICC) session was held in Bombay in the Gowalia Tank Maidan, opposite the Goculdas Tejpal House where the Indian National Congress had been established in 1885. On 7 August about 10,000 persons attended the meeting. Another 5000 were outside the *pandal* listening to Gandhi. In his speech that day Gandhi stressed the importance of non-violence:

AICC in session, Mumbai, August 1942

With Mahadev Desai in AICC meeting, Mumbai, August 1942

In AICC meeting with Pandit Jawaharlal Nehru and Acharya J.B. Kripalani, Mumbai, August 1942

Drafting the resolution

> At a time when I am about to launch the biggest fight in my life there can be no hatred for the British in my heart... Non-violence is a matchless weapon which can help everyone ... if you want real freedom you will have to come together and such coming together will create true democracy ... I want you to adopt non-violence as a matter of policy. With me it is a creed... As disciplined soldiers you must accept it in toto and stick to it when you join the struggle.[48]

On 8 August, about the same number of people were in the *pandal* and outside. Anticipating that Congress leaders may be arrested, Gandhi declared in his passionate 'Do or Die' speech,

> Every one of you who desires freedom and strives for it must be his own guide... Every one of you from this moment onwards consider yourself a free man or woman and act as if you are free ... I am not going to be satisfied with anything short of freedom. We shall do or die. We shall either free India or die in the attempt.[49]

In an interview to the *Bombay Chronicle* on 8 August, Gandhi said that if the resolution was passed, 'I shall be the chief actor in the tragedy; it is therefore dreadful if any Englishman considers me to be guilty of hatred for the British ... I own no enemy on earth. That is my creed.'[50]

It was announced that a flag salutation would take place on Sunday, 9 August, at the Gowalia Tank Maidan in the morning, followed by an address by Jawaharlal Nehru. Gandhi was to address a public meeting In Shivaji Park in Dadar.

However, in the early morning of 9 August, Gandhi and all members of the Congress Working Committee were arrested to pre-empt the movement from succeeding. This marked the beginning of the Quit India Movement.

Gandhi, Miraben and Mahadev Desai were taken to Aga Khan Palace in Poona. The members of the Congress Working Committee were taken to Ahmednagar Fort and the Bombay Congress leaders were sent to Yeravda Jail.

Kasturba offered to take Gandhi's place at the Shivaji park meeting. On the way, she and Dr Sushila Nayyar were stopped by the police who pleaded with them not to proceed. One lakh people who had assembled at Shivaji Park went wild with enthusiasm to see Kasturba, but she and Dr Sushila Nayyar were arrested and taken to Arthur Road Prison in Bombay. They were later shifted to Aga Khan Palace.

Women protesters on march

FACING PAGE Women *satyagrahis* bravely facing the police

When the Congress leaders were whisked away to prison, Aruna Asaf Ali unfurled the national flag at the Gowalia Tank Maidan. The meeting was declared illegal under Section 144. As soon as the flag was unfurled the police lobbed tear gas shells into the crowd and curfew was imposed.

Unlike the Non-Cooperation and Civil Disobedience movements, there was no definite programme this time. Gandhi's instructions to civil resisters that were discussed in the Working Committee were an outline of the programme of the Quit India Movement. But they were rather vague and general. He told every Congressman that he was his own leader. All students above the age of 16 should come out of their schools and colleges and not return till independence. People should refuse to pay taxes, land revenue and other government dues. 'The object of the struggle was to

Women's procession during Quit India Movement
FACING PAGE Press clippings of Quit India Movement

secure the withdrawal of the British rule and attainment of independence for the whole of India.' This included every activity in a mass movement.[51]

As news of these arrests spread, spontaneous *hartal*s took place all over the country. There were processions, meetings and demonstrations in defiance of the law. Tear gas and *lathi* charge were used to stop the protesters. Protests were not just confined to the cities. As the news spread into the rural areas, the villagers also joined. For the first six or seven weeks after 9 August, there was a tremendous mass upsurge all over the country. In some places crowds attacked police stations, post offices, courts and railway stations. Small groups of people blew up railway bridges, removed railway tracks, cut telephone and telegraph wires. In Gujarat, women stored bombs, acid and small arms in their homes for blowing up railway stations or cutting off telegraph lines. Students went on strike in schools and colleges. In Ahmedabad, mill workers went on strike for three and a half months. Workers in Bombay also stayed away from work for a week. So did workers in Jamshedpur.

In Assam, Kanaklata Barua, a young girl in her teens, led a procession of five hundred and was shot dead in police firing.

A new feature of the Quit India Movement was the emergence of 'parallel governments' in some parts of the country. In Bengal, Midnapur was once again the most active district. A 'national' or 'parallel' government called Tamralipta Jatiya Sarkar was formed in Tamluk. It had its own army called vidyut vahini. Peasants protested against taxes, land tenure and landholders' rights. They attacked police stations and destroyed telegraph lines. Police repression

TOP Police trying to disperse the protesting crowd
ABOVE Protest in front of police

followed and there was considerable violence. The people of Tamluk sub-division marched towards the town intending to capture the court and police station. Armed soldiers were guarding the court and the crowd hesitated to move forward. Matangini Hazra, a woman of 73, went forward, lifted the tricolor flag and gave her first public lecture. She asked the people to go forward in the name of Mahatma Gandhi. The police started beating her but she refused to loosen her grip on the flag. They fired a bullet at her hand and then at her head. She fell down and died. Despite official efforts to crush the revolt, the people of Midnapur continued their resistance.[52]

The first of these parallel governments was set up in Ballia in Eastern U.P. under Chittu Pande in August 1942. The most successful was the one formed in Satara in Maharashtra, where Y.B. Chavan was the most important leader.

In Bombay, among the leaders of the movement were Yusuf Meherally, B.G. Kher, S.K. Patil, Shankarrao Deo, Achyut Patwardhan and Ashok Mehta.

One of the most dramatic episodes in Bombay was the Congress Radio that gave regular bulletins of national and international news. The courageous core group of Usha Mehta, Vithaldas and Chandrakant Jhaveri was helped by leaders like Ram Manohar Lohia and others. The radio had its own transmitter, recording station, call sign and a distinct wave length. When the press was gagged and news of the movement banned, this radio helped in broadcasting news about the movement. To prevent from getting caught by the police, they kept changing their places of transmission. The Congress Radio lasted from 14 August until the 12 November 1942 when police raided the

Subhas Chandra Bose inspecting the Indian National Army soldiers with Captain Laxmi

place of transmission and arrested Chandrakant Jhaveri and Usha Mehta on the spot. They were charged with 'working illegally and disturbing the government'. Usha Mehta and Chandrakant Jhaveri were sentenced for four years and one year respectively. Usha Mehta was sent to Yervada jail in Poona, kept in a solitary cell for two months, and interrogated daily.[53]

The movement became almost like a revolt in Bihar and Eastern U.P. Students of Benares Hindu University went to the villages to spread the message of Quit India. They

Gandhi with Maulana Abul Kalam Azad, Acharya J.B. Kripalani and Sadiq Ali at an AICC meeting, Mumbai

FACING PAGE With Sardar Vallabhbhai Patel, Mumbai, August 1942

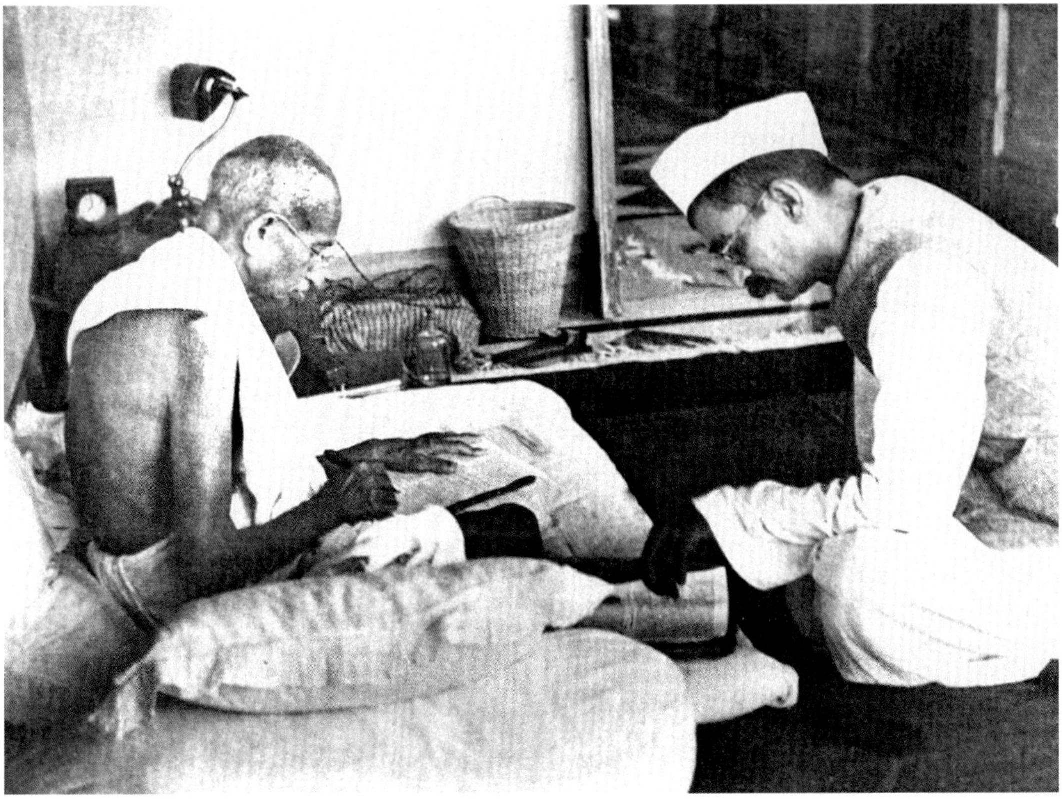

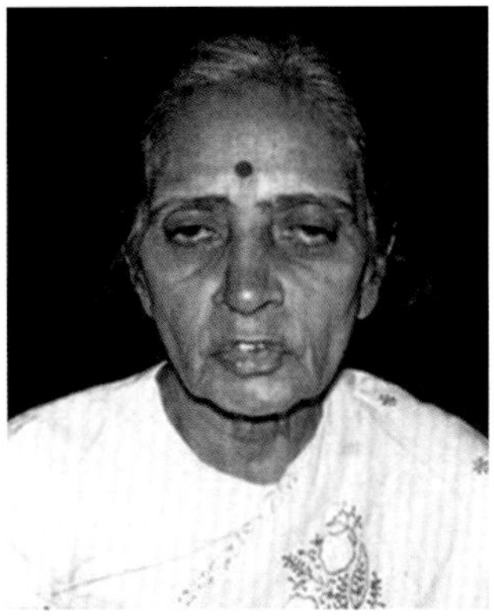

TOP With Dr Rajendra Prasad, Mumbai, August 1942

RIGHT Usha Mehta

FACING PAGE Gandhi with Abul Kalam Azad, Mumbai, August 1942

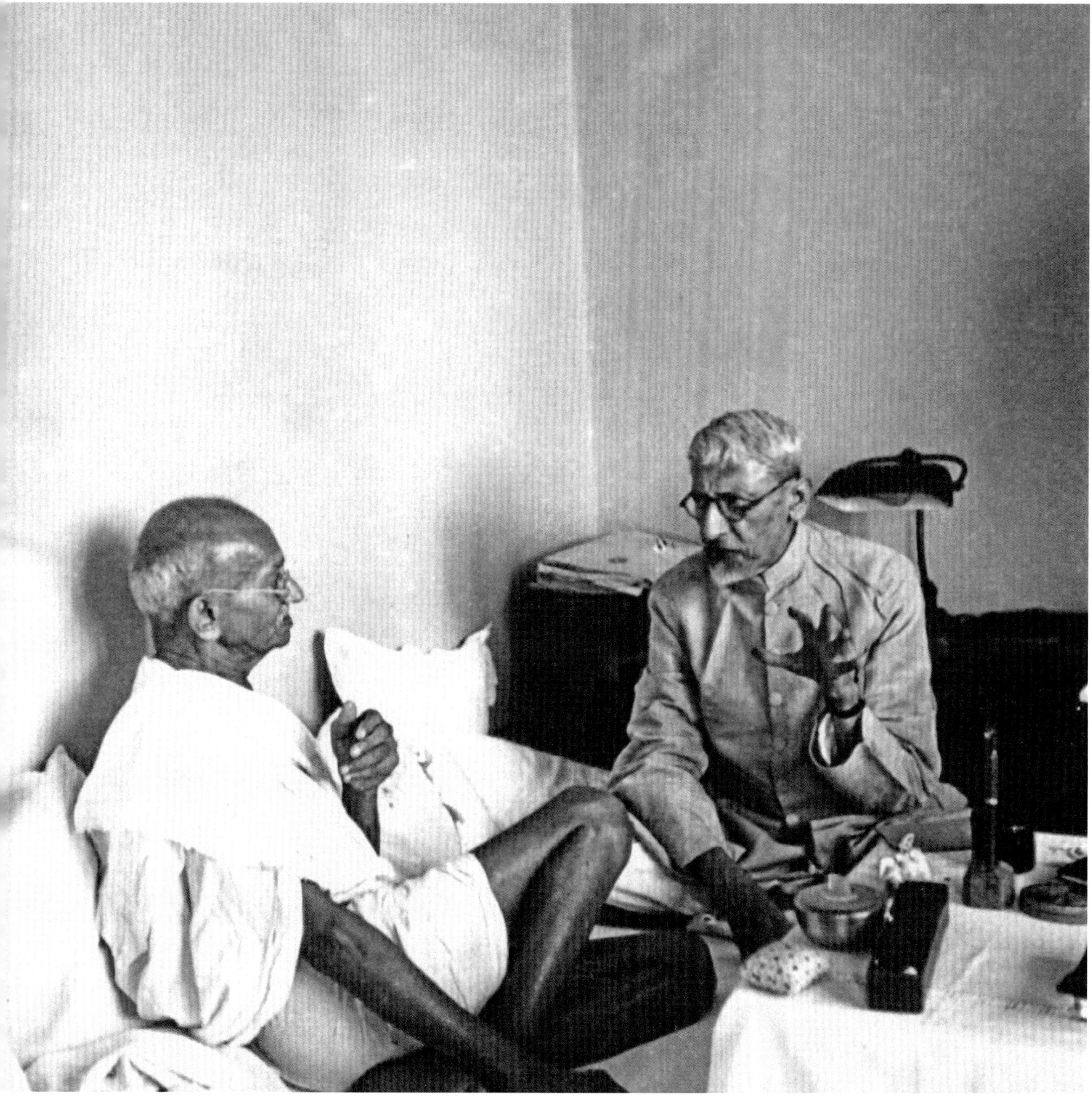

hijacked trains and draped them in national flags. They raised slogans of '*thana jalao*' (burn police stations), '*station phoonk do*' (burn the railway station) and '*angrez bhag gaya*' (Englishmen have fled). Government responded by firing and repression. For two weeks the Tirhut Division of Bihar was cut off from the rest of the country and there was no government authority. Important centres of resistance were Azamgarh, Ballia, and Gorakhpur in Eastern U.P. and Gaya, Bhagalpur, Purnea, Champaran, Saran, Muzaffarpur and Shahbad in Bihar.

In Delhi also, men and women marched in processions, held meetings, picketed shops and courted arrest. Among the prominent women who took part was Satyavati Devi (granddaughter of Swami Shraddhanand) who was arrested and kept as a security prisoner. She worked among the textile workers of Delhi.

Delhi University students also took part. In 1942, soon after his arrest when Gandhi went on a fast in Aga Khan Palace, students and teachers of Delhi University took out a prayer procession led by Professor V.K.R.V. Rao. Ajit Bhattacharya, a renowned journalist recalled, that on 10 August, a 'Vociferous gathering of Hinduites and ladies from Indraprastha College gathered outside the gates of St Stephen's and urged Stephanians to join them in the procession to support the Congress leaders who had been jailed the previous day. The crowd marched down Alipur Road, passing *en route* I.P. College whose authorities had shut the gates to prevent the remaining girls from joining in. They resourcefully jumped down the walls, assisted by willing Stephanian hands, and the procession continued down to Chandni Chowk shouting slogans.'[54]

According to official estimates, in the first week after 9 August, 250 railway stations were damaged or destroyed and over 500 post offices and 150 police stations were attacked. By the end of 1942, over 60,000 people were arrested.[55]

The all round repression was successful in suppressing the mass phase of the movement within six to seven weeks. But in the meantime, an underground movement was developing under the leadership of Achyut Patwardhan, Ram Manohar Lohia, Aruna Asaf Ali, Sucheta Kripalani, Biju Patnaik and others. Jayaprakash Narayan joined this group after his escape from jail. They tried to keep the movement alive by distributing money as well as bombs, arms and dynamite to underground groups. Local underground organisations were active in Bombay, Poona, Satara, Baroda, and some parts of Gujarat, U.P., Bihar, Andhra, Karnataka, Kerala and Delhi.

Aruna Asaf Ali was one of the most important figures of the 1942 underground movement. A warrant was issued for her arrest, but she moved from place to place and avoided being arrested and kept the movement alive. The All India Women's Conference journal *Roshni* described her as the 'direct successor of Devi Chaudhurani', the dacoit queen, who robbed the rich and gave to the poor.[56] She worked closely with other underground leaders, published bulletins and edited with Ram Manohar Lohia a monthly magazine of the Congress party, *Inquilab*. Yusuf Meherally wrote, 'If the heroine of 1857 was the Rani of Jhansi, that of 1942 revolution was undoubtedly Aruna Asaf Ali.'[57]

Sucheta Kripalani also played an important role in the underground movement. She, together with Ram Manohar Lohia, Achyut Patwardhan, Sadiq Ali and others, formed a Central Directorate whose task was to keep in contact with

LEFT TO RIGHT
Ram Manohar Lohia

Jayaprakash Narayan

Aruna Asaf Ali

FACING PAGE Achyut Patwardhan

Mahatma Gandhi in front of his hut out for a morning walk,
Juhu, Mumbai, June 1944

underground groups active in different parts of the country. They organised derailment of trains, bomb outrages, circulation of illegal pamphlets and holding demonstrations. Later, the group split into a non-violent group led by Sucheta and a pro-violence group led by Jayaprakash Narayan. Sucheta resigned from the Central Directorate and formed a new group called the All India Satyagraha Council. She avoided being arrested by travelling from province to province in disguise, but was finally arrested in 1944 and kept in Lucknow jail as a 'dangerous person'.[58]

In terms of popular participation, the Quit India Movement marked a new phase. As in the earlier movements, students played a significant role, so did women. Businessmen and industrialists gave financial support. Peasants and simple villagers gave shelter to underground workers and protected them by refusing to divulge information as did ordinary people in cities. Gandhi's release in 1944 on grounds of ill health brought the movement to an end.

Mahatma Gandhi on his morning walk,
Rashtriyashala, Rajkot, Gujarat, March 1939

Walking Alone and Freedom

EKLA CHALO—NOAKHALI

With the surrender of Japan on 15 August 1945, the Second World War ended. In the elections held a month before, the Labour Party headed by Clement Attlee came to power. One of the first steps the new government took was to hold a general election in India which had been last held in 1936. Congress secured 93.3 per cent of the votes in the Central Legislative Assembly, in the general constituencies, and in the Provincial Legislatures, it won absolute majorities in Bombay, Madras United Provinces, Bihar, Orissa and Central Provinces. In the North West Provinces, it won 30 seats while the Muslim League got only 17. While the Muslim League won every Muslim seat in the Central Legislature, it secured a majority only Bengal and Sind. In March, the Cabinet Mission was sent to India but after prolonged negotiations its plan was rejected both by the Congress and the League.

In 1946, a year before India became independent, Hindu-Muslim tension flared up in different parts of the country. On 16 August, Calcutta witnessed communal riots, the scale and intensity of which was unparalleled. The Muslim League declared it is as 'Direct Action Day' to record its protest against the Cabinet Mission's recommendations. This led to a communal holocaust in Calcutta as the League was in power there. Crowds went on a rampage, killing, looting and indulging in rape and arson. The events in Calcutta came to be known as the 'Great Calcutta Killing'.

Gandhi was in Sevagram when he learnt about the riots in Calcutta. He said, 'Calcutta has given us an ocular demonstration of what Direct Action is and how it is done.' He went to Delhi and for the next two months was busy in the political negotiations.

In the first week of October, news came of ghastly communal riots in Noakhali. Local *goonda*s had burnt the property of Hindus, looted their crops, desecrated their temples, and what hurt and disturbed Gandhi most was that they had kidnapped and raped their women. He cancelled all his plans and decided to leave for East Bengal. Throughout his life, he always wanted first to acquaint himself with the prevailing situation, know all the facts, before intervening. He announced on 27 October that he was proceeding to Calcutta the next day on his way to Noakhali. Friends tried to dissuade him as his health was poor and important negotiations were going on for which his advice would be required. But he was determined to go. 'I do not know what I shall be able to do there. All that I know is that I won't be at

‘Walking alone’— in Noakhali, 1946

Gandhi with British Parliamentry delegration, Madras, 1946

FACING PAGE Gandhi with Pathick Lawrance, a member of the Cabinet Mission, Delhi, 1946

peace unless I go', he said. 'I am going to console and wipe the tears of grief stricken men and women. I shall try to instill courage and fortitude in their sinking hearts. I shall not judge any one. My only object is to serve the people, to work for peace and amity between the two communities. Born in the same country, Hindus and Muslims have lived together for long. They can never be enemies of each other. Can religious differences ever disapprove this simple truth?'[59]

Gandhi while moving towards a riot affected village, sharing a word with accompanying women group, Noakhali, 1947

FACING PAGE Gandhi riding on a boat while going to a riot affected village in Noakhali, 1946

In Calcutta, he saw the ravages of the August riots and confessed to a 'sinking feeling' at the mass madness which can turn man into nothing less than a brute. Nirmal Kumar Bose became Gandhi's interpreter and Gandhi asked him to read all the local newspapers and collect all the relevant material. Gandhi got his entourage together and proceeded to Noakhali, a remote inaccessible place, located in the water logged delta of the Ganga and the Brahmaputra. Apart from N.K. Bose, the team included Pyarelal, Dr Sushila Nayyar, Kanu and Abha Gandhi and Parasuram.

Gandhi riding on a boat while going to a riot affected village in Noakhali, 1946

FACING PAGE Gandhi seen in the motor launch carrying him to Contai during his peace mission in Bengal, 1946

Gandhi in Mahishadal, Bengal, 1946

Gandhi found the atmosphere in East Bengal charged with fear, hatred and violence. Truth and non-violence by which he had sworn for sixty years seemed to have failed to show the attributes he had ascribed to them. To test them and himself, he rose at 4 am and walked barefooted from village to village and saw for himself burnt houses and heard stories of looting and forcible conversion. In the village of Kazirkhil, Gandhi decided to live in a Muslim household as he hoped that if the Hindus saw him living with a Muslim family they might feel confident to return. He then went to a tiny village of Shrirampur to test *ahimsa* and truth, 'or better to test myself'. He stayed there for some time to consolidate his peace mission. Many of Gandhi's co-workers lived in villages doing work of rescue and rehabilitation which gradually began to show some result.

Pyarelal came to Shrirampur and met Gandhi to find out the meaning of 'do or die'. He saw Gandhi trying to cross a rivulet which was spanned by a bridge consisting of a few bamboo logs tied together. Gandhi tried to cross several times, but could not do so without the support of N.K. Bose. After seven or eight times, he finally managed to cross on his own. This was his explanation of 'do or die'.

Gandhi went from village to village, door to door to explain his mission. During his walking tour, he turned his prayer meetings into question-answer sessions. This was partly to explain his position and partly to increase interaction with the people. Nehru urged him to come to Delhi but a sense of loneliness overwhelmed him and he felt that his political associates were drifting away. To G.D. Birla, he wrote: 'I have to consider where my place is. My voice carries no weight in the Working Committee. Is it really time for me to retire to the Himalayas?'[60]

Gandhi was in Bengal for four months. His walking tour in Noakhali covered 56 villages and a total distance of 116 miles. To him the whole thing was a pilgrimage. As he said, 'His barefoot walk need not provide sensation. Pilgrimage was always performed barefoot. For him this tour was a pilgrimage pure and simple.'[61] He wanted to restore the 'intrinsic trust' between Hindus and Muslims.

Was Gandhi's mission in Noakhali successful? This is not an easy question to answer. The attendance at his prayer meetings varied from village to village and reached its peak at Paniala village where nearly five thousand people gathered.[62] In some villages, inter-communal dinners were held. When objections were raised to the singing of *ram dhun*, Gandhi explained that Rama, Khuda, Ishwar were all names of God. In fact God is known by a million names.[63]

According to B.R. Nanda, 'Gandhi's presence acted as a soothing balm in the villages of East Bengal, it eased tensions, assuaged anger and softened tempers. His success would have been more spectacular were it not for the sustained propaganda against him in the Muslim press.'[64]

Gandhi himself said that those who wanted to know if the situation had improved or not should ask those who had suffered. 'Personally I feel that the situation has improved and there is more self confidence among the people today…'.[65]

PILGRIMAGE FOR PEACE—BIHAR

In November 1946, communal riots had broken out in Bihar in retaliation for what had happened in Calcutta and Noakhali. About three and a half lakh Muslims had fled Bihar; men and women had been brutally killed and even children had not been spared. Over 400 villages were destroyed. While he was in Noakhali, numerous appeals were made to Gandhi that he was needed in Bihar. He wrote to Dr Syed Mahmud asking for full details. He also sent Sardar Niranjan Singh Gill of the Indian National Army, who had been working with him in Noakhali, to go there and give him a first-hand account of the situation. In March 1947, in response to desperate appeals for help, and a letter from Dr Syed Mahmud, Gandhi left for Bihar to assess the situation, hoping to restore sanity. He was accompanied by Mridula Sarabhai, Khan Abdul Gaffar Khan, Professor Nirmal Kumar Bose, Manu Gandhi, Dev Prakash (brother of Pyarelal), the photographer Jagan Mehta, and Hamid Hunnar, Gandhi's Hindi translator.

Gandhi had planned to be in Bihar for only seven or ten days.

> Muslim League leaders and workers had been sending him reports about the condition in Bihar, that though five months had elapsed since the riots, the atmosphere was as tense as a live volcano, that ruined dwellings still stood in the same condition as reminders of man's beastliness, the plight of the refugees was getting worse day by day, the Hindus were becoming more aggressive and everywhere lawlessness prevailed.[66]

Gandhi could not believe that all these reports were true. He arrived in Bihar hoping that, as had happened with the Pirpur Report of 1939–40, most of the complaints would prove to be exaggerated, and that after the rehabilitation programme launched by the Bihar government, there would be little for him to do.

Gandhi accompanied by Mridula Sarabhai, Abha Gandhi, Khan Abdul Gaffar Khan

FACING PAGE (BOTH)
Gandhi and Mridula Sarabhai visiting the riot affected areas in Bihar, 1947

Walking with Mridula Sarabhai at Patna, outside his local camp, Bihar, 1947

A motorcar accompanied and when Gandhi got tired
he got into the car, Bihar, 1947

On his morning walk with Khan Abdul Ghaffar Khan
and Abha Gandhi, Bihar, 1947

On the first day, in his prayer speech, he said, 'Arriving here, I saw that we had indeed committed a great sin. ... This is the way of obstructing the country's freedom ... I said in Noakhali that I would "do or die" there. That applies in Bihar, too. If our thoughts are not good, our actions too will not be good...'[67] He said,

> Bihar made me known to the whole of India. Before that, very few in the country had heard of me. My coming to Champaran woke up the whole country. I felt as if the people of Bihar and I had known each other for ages. In short, I felt as if Bihar was my own province. Bihar showed me my way. I taught Bihar the weapon of satyagraha.[68]

Gandhi was staying in Dr Syed Mahmud's residence on the banks of the Ganga. There was a continuous stream of visitors from morning to evening, Hindus and Muslims, old and young, rich and poor either wanted to pour out their tragic stories or simply have his *darshan*. Refugee women in *purdah* came to see him. One of them said in a tear choked voice, 'So you are that Gandhi, with whose name on their lips they killed my grandson in my lap. Tell us what should we do? ... What harm have we done? ... How did our Hindu neighbours who used to address our men as uncles, go so mad? Why have they ruined us?'[69] Such heart rending stories filled Gandhi with indescribable pain .

Gandhi's prayer speeches reflected the state of his mind. He urged people to behave decently, not out of fear of law, but out of simple human duty. He made efforts to remove fear from the hearts of Muslims and win their trust.

Talking to a riot victim in Bihar, 1947

Gandhi on a walking tour in riot affected area, Bihar, 1947

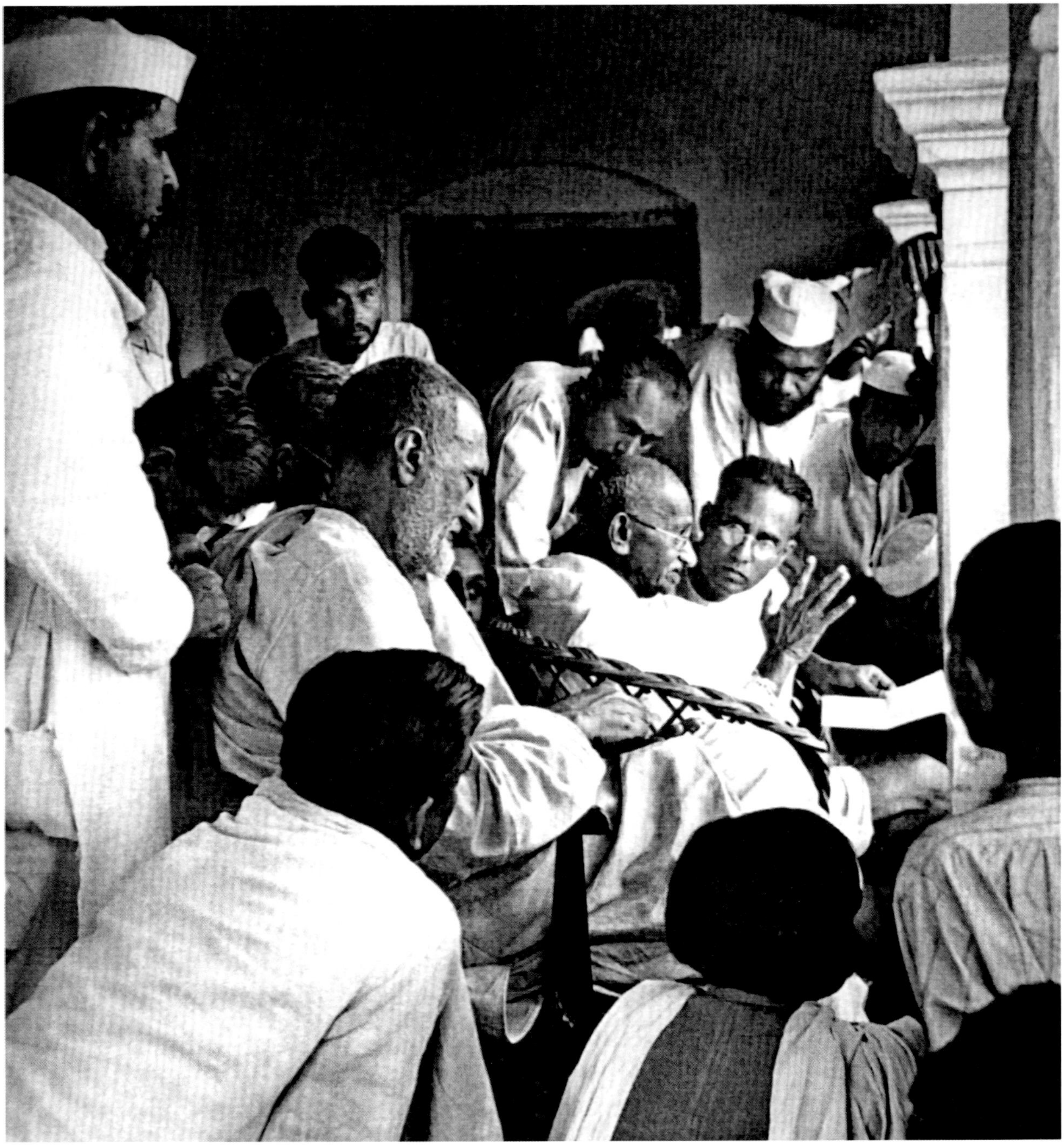

At a public meeting in Ghosi, Bihar, March 1947

The prayer speeches had a miraculous effect. The residents of a village called Sipara wrote a letter apologising for what they had done and assured Gandhi that they would try to persuade the Muslims of the village who had fled to return to their homes. He told the people: 'If you betray my faith in you and a single Muslim is assaulted, Bihar and India will lose Gandhi.'

12 March 1930 was the historic day of the Dandi March. After seventeen years, on the same day, Gandhi began a tour of Bihar villages. He had toured Noakhali villages on foot to instill courage into the hearts of terrified Hindus. He walked in Orissa to atone for the inhuman treatment of *harijan*s by caste Hindus. After considerable persuasion, Gandhi agreed to undertake the tour of Bihar by train and car. From six to eight o'clock in the mornings and four to seven or eight in the afternoon and evenings he visited the villages. Prayer meetings were arranged in several places on each day as people in all the villages wanted to see and hear him. Certain hours were reserved for meeting visitors. Gandhi wanted to investigate every complaint himself and satisfy himself in every detail.

Instead of his original plan of staying only for a week or so in Bihar, Gandhi spent two months to get a first-hand idea of the destruction during the riots and the problems of rehabilitation. Seventy-six-year-old Gandhi's ardous tour through hundreds of miles of difficult terrain, often walking barefooted, was truly amazing. He regarded this as a pilgrimage. Later on in *Harijan*, he described this tour as 'the supreme test of the efficacy of the idea of non-violence'.

Speaking in a meeting while reassuring that he is ready to give up his life for communal harmony, Bihar, 1946

Hydari Manzil, Beliaghata, where Gandhi stayed on 15 August 1947

Nehru hoisting the national flag at Red Fort on 15 August 1947

Freedom at Midnight

Prime Minister Attlee announced in February 1947, in the House of Commons, that the British would quit India after transferring power into responsible hands not later than June 1948. He also announced the appointment of Lord Mountbatten as Viceroy in place of Lord Wavell. Mountbatten arrived in March and immediately began talks for the transfer of power. Shortly after this, the Muslim League escalated communal violence in Punjab which led to the downfall of the non-League coalition ministry and the League once again called for a 'Direct Action Day'. The renewed communal violence convinced Mountbatten that partition was the only answer. Gandhi was vehemently opposed to this idea and had declared that 'if the Congress wishes to accept partition it will be over my dead body. So long as I am alive, I will never agree to the partition of India.' But in the prevailing atmosphere, Congress leaders,

Constituent Assembly meeting at the Council House Library, New Delhi, 1947

especially Nehru and Patel, who had the experience of working with the League in the Interim Government, agreed with Mountbatten, that partition was the only choice.

All this time Gandhi was in Bihar on his Peace Mission. He came to Delhi on 31 March 1947, met the Viceroy, leaders of the Congress and other political parties. He was receiving letters saying that he was a slave of Jinnah and a fifth columnist playing false to the Hindus. He came to terms with the partition. He did not want to stay in Delhi and announced his desire to go back to Bihar. The Constituent Assembly met on the night of 14 August 1947 and Jawaharlal Nehru in his unforgettable address said, 'At the stroke of the midnight hour, when the world sleeps, India will awake to life and freedom'. Independence was achieved but it was accompanied by communal hatred and violence, the kind of which India had never seen before.

Jawaharlal Nehru addressing the Constituent Assembly
on 14 August 1947, at midnight

Nehru taking oath as Prime Minister of Interim Government

I had the rare privilege of witnessing the historic Transfer of Power Ceremony on the midnight of 14–15 August 1947, as my father was a member of the Constituent Assembly and as such was allowed to take one guest.

The ceremony was held in the magnificent high domed Central Legislative Hall (now Parliament House). The room was brilliantly lit and decorated with flags. Proceedings began with the singing of *Vande Mataram* and a two minutes silence was observed for those who had died in the country's freedom struggle. Here were four speakers— Dr Rajendra Prasad, Chaudhry Khaliquzzaman, Dr Radahakrishnan, and Jawaharlal Nehru, who in his inimitable manner and emotion-choked voice made the memorable speech: 'At the stroke of the midnight hour, when the world sleeps, India will awake to life and freedom.'

Exactly at midnight, conches were blown and a cry of 'Mahatma Gandhi ki jai' echoed through the hall. A group of women sang *Sare Jahan Se Accha Hindustsn Hamara* and *Jana Gana Mana*. Representing the women of India, a group of them formally presented the national flag to the Assembly. As we came out of the hall, there were thousands outside shouting 'Inquilab Zindabad', 'Mahatma Gandhi ki jai' and 'Jawaharlal Nehru ki jai', and it was almost impossible to move.

Though this was more than 70 years ago, one treasures such memories. I feel that, 'It was bliss in that dawn to be alive but to be young was very heaven.'

—Aparna Basu

THE MIRACLE OF CALCUTTA

On 9 August Gandhi arrived in Calcutta. He meant to go to Noakhali, but events in Calcutta forced him to stay there. Since the riots of August 1946, Calcutta had remained paralysed with communal hatred and fear. In March 1947, once again communal riots broke out which lasted for four days. When Gandhi arrived in Calcutta in August the situation was still tense. Mohammad Usman, Secretary of the Calcutta Muslim League met Gandhi and urged him to stay in Calcutta for two more days. Gandhi said that he would do so only if the League guaranteed peace in Noakhali.[70] He threatened that he would go on a fast if there was any communal violence in Noakhali.

Suhrawardy, the Chief Minister of Bengal also urged Gandhi to stay on. Gandhi agreed saying, 'if you and I are prepared to live together, we shall have to work as long as every Hindu and Muslim in Calcutta does not return to the place he was before.'[71] Suhrawardy agreed to Gandhi's proposal. The place chosen for them to stay was 150 Beliaghata Road, an old rambling building which was locally called Hydari Mansion.

When he arrived at Hydari Mansion many said, 'Last year when Direct Action was launched on August 16 you did not come.' Gandhi replied, 'I accept that all the atrocities of August 16 (1946) were perpetrated… by Muslims. But what is the use of avenging past wrongs? I have not come for the good of Muslims alone. I want to serve everybody, for I am a friend of all men.'[72]

Young men came and argued with Gandhi. He told them that his aim was to restore communal harmony.

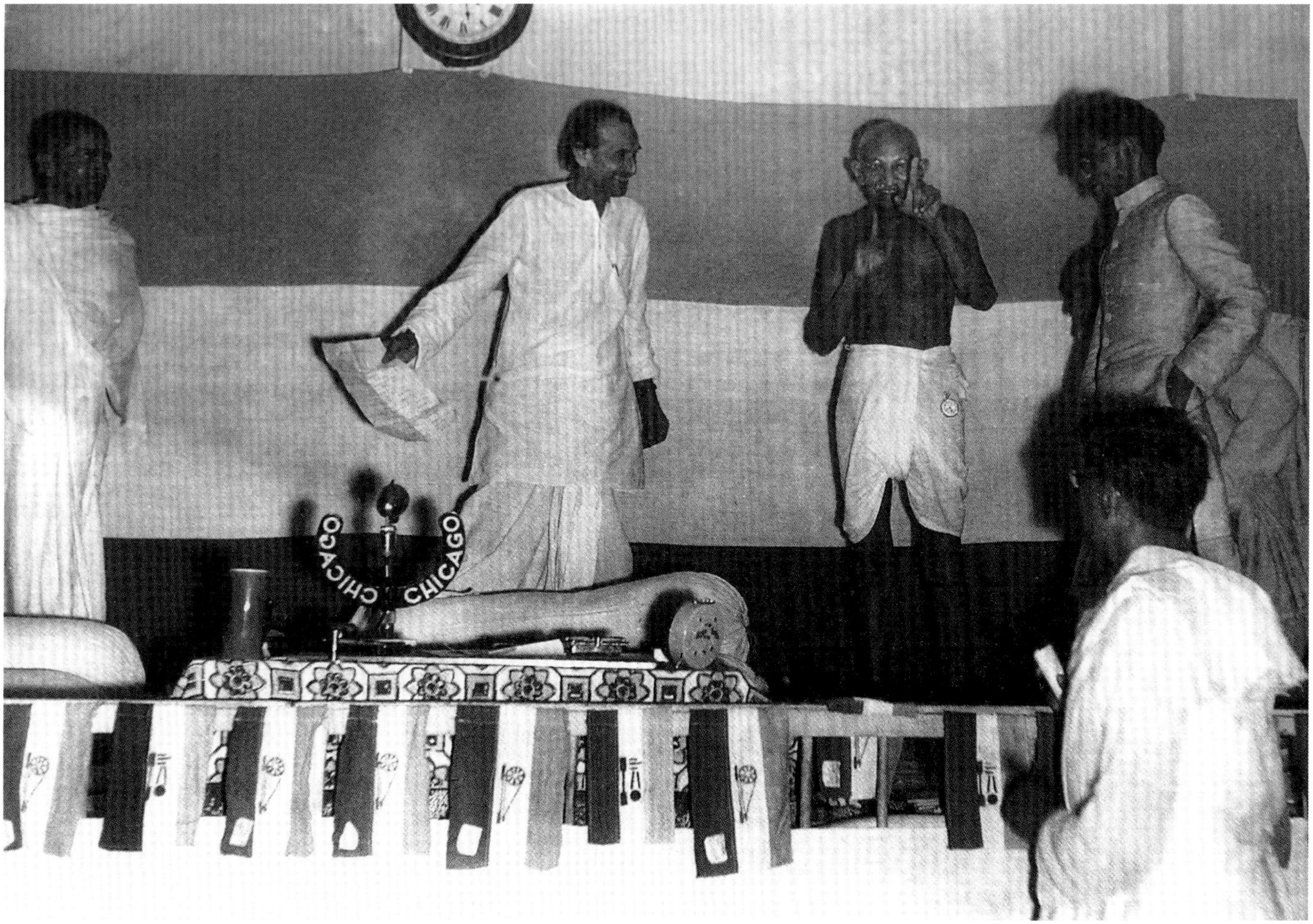

Gandhi at the Working Committee meeting, June 1947

Gandhiji during his fast in Calcutta, September 1947

In his after prayer speech on 14 August, Gandhi spoke of independence and partition. 'Tomorrow will thus be a day of rejoicing as well as mourning. If communal strife spreads over the whole of India, of what use is our freedom?'[73]

15 August 1947 was a historic day for millions of Indians. Yet for the chief architect of the freedom movement, it was a sad day. It was the fifth death anniversary of his closest associate Mahadev Desai. Independence Day was celebrated by Gandhi by fasting. He had the entire Gita recited to him in memory of Mahadevbhai. He had been invited to Delhi to

Speaking with Hindu and Muslim representatives,
Calcutta, September 1947

Refugees from Punjab (Pakistan), 1947

participate in the celebrations, but he declined preferring to stay in Calcutta to restore communal harmony.

A day earlier he had asked for armed guards to be removed from Hydari Mansion and replaced by Hindu and Muslim volunteers. His Muslim hosts decorated the house with tricolor. In the early hours of the morning, a group of young girls arrived singing Rabindranath Tagore's songs. They stood outside the window of Gandhi's room, stopped singing and joined the prayer going on inside.

In the afternoon, Gandhi walked to a nearby *maidan* in Beliaghata for a prayer meeting. Hindus and Muslims were present and he shouted, 'Hindu Muslim *ek ho*' .

Lord Mountbatten said that, in 'Punjab we have fifty five thousand soldiers and large scale rioting on our hands ... in Bengal our forces consist of one man, and there is no rioting.'[74]

The real orgy of communal violence was taking place in Punjab. Many requested him to go there. Nehru wrote saying Punjab needed his 'healing touch', but Gandhi was keen on going to Noakhali. His presence in Calcutta on 15 August 1947 contributed to the peace in Calcutta and served as 'an abject lesson in the neighbourliness which is the only true answer to communal fury'.[75]

Mountbatten wrote to Gandhi on 26 August, 'As a serving officer, as well as an administrator may I be allowed to pay my tribute to the one man boundary force, not forgetting his second-in-command, Mr. Suhrawardy?'[76]

Violence erupted in Calcutta at the end of August. The communal holocaust in Punjab inflamed passions. By 1 September, rioting had spread all over the city. In an incident close to Hydari Mansion, some workmen were killed when

With C. Rajagopalachari, Mumbai, August 1942

hand grenades were thrown on the truck in which they were travelling. On hearing the explosion, Gandhi walked to the scene with Manuben and N.K. Bose. For a long time he gazed at the dead bodies. The intensity of the violence shook Gandhi and he resolved to undertake a fast unto death. Rajagopalachari argued with Gandhi that it was no use fasting against *goondas*. Gandhi replied that his aim was to touch the hearts of those who were behind the *goondas*.

Many people came to meet Gandhi during his fast. Prafulla Chandra Ghosh, who had become the first Chief Minister of Bengal in independent India, complained that Gandhi had undertaken the fast without consulting his cabinet and that Hindus felt that the fast was against them. Gandhi said that was not true.[77]

When Dr Shyama Prasad Mookerjee of the Hindu Mahasabha came to see him, Gandhi told him that he would break his fast when he reported that all was quiet in Calcutta. Gandhi's message to everyone was that they should go in the midst of the riots and prevent the rioters from indulging in madness.

The Calcutta police undertook a twenty four hour sympathetic fast. This, together with rigorous military action stemmed the violence. On 4 September several *goonda*s and gang leaders of both communities came to Beliaghata and surrendered their knives and Sten guns and confessed their crimes.

To all those who came urging him to give up his fast, his message was 'go out and protect the Muslims'. 'The minute I am convinced that a real change of heart has taken place, I will give up my fast.'[78]

It was only after prominent citizens and politicians of Calcutta signed a pledge promising not to allow any recurrence of communal violence, that Gandhi agreed to break his fast. It had lasted seventy-three hours. Rajaji called it a 'victory over evil' for Gandhi. People continued to come to surrender weapons.

On 7 September 1947, Gandhi left for Delhi. It was in Calcutta that Gandhi wrote to Devtosh Gupta of the Shanti Sena Dal in Bengal, 'My life is my message'.[79]

There can be no other appropriate ending to this episode than a letter written to the editor of the *Statesman* in 1947: 'I have always had great respect for Mr. Gandhi, but could not make up my mind to speak of him as Mahatma. However, seeing the wonders he has done in Calcutta, I have no hesitation now in doing so. I hope you will take the same view and in future write Mahatma Gandhi and not Mr. Gandhi.'[80]

Gandhi at a prayer meeting, Delhi, July 1947

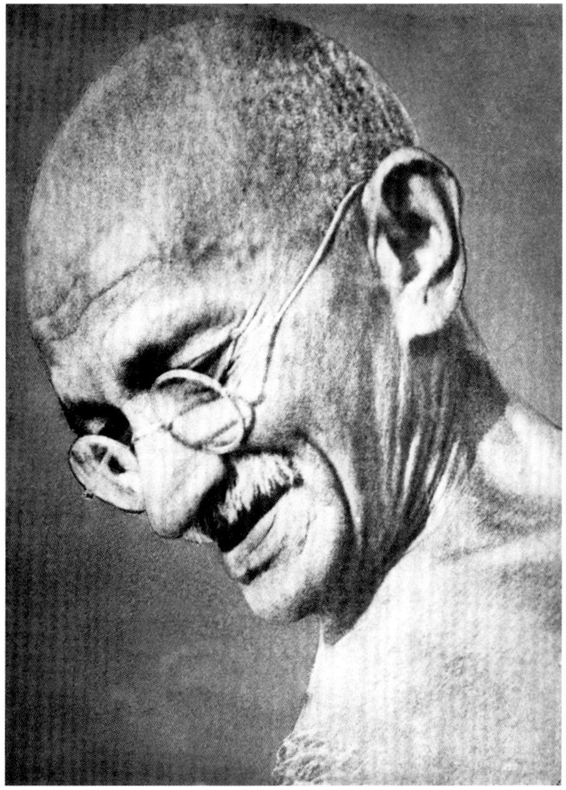

Mahatma Gandhi, 1938

Gandhi's Dream of Free India

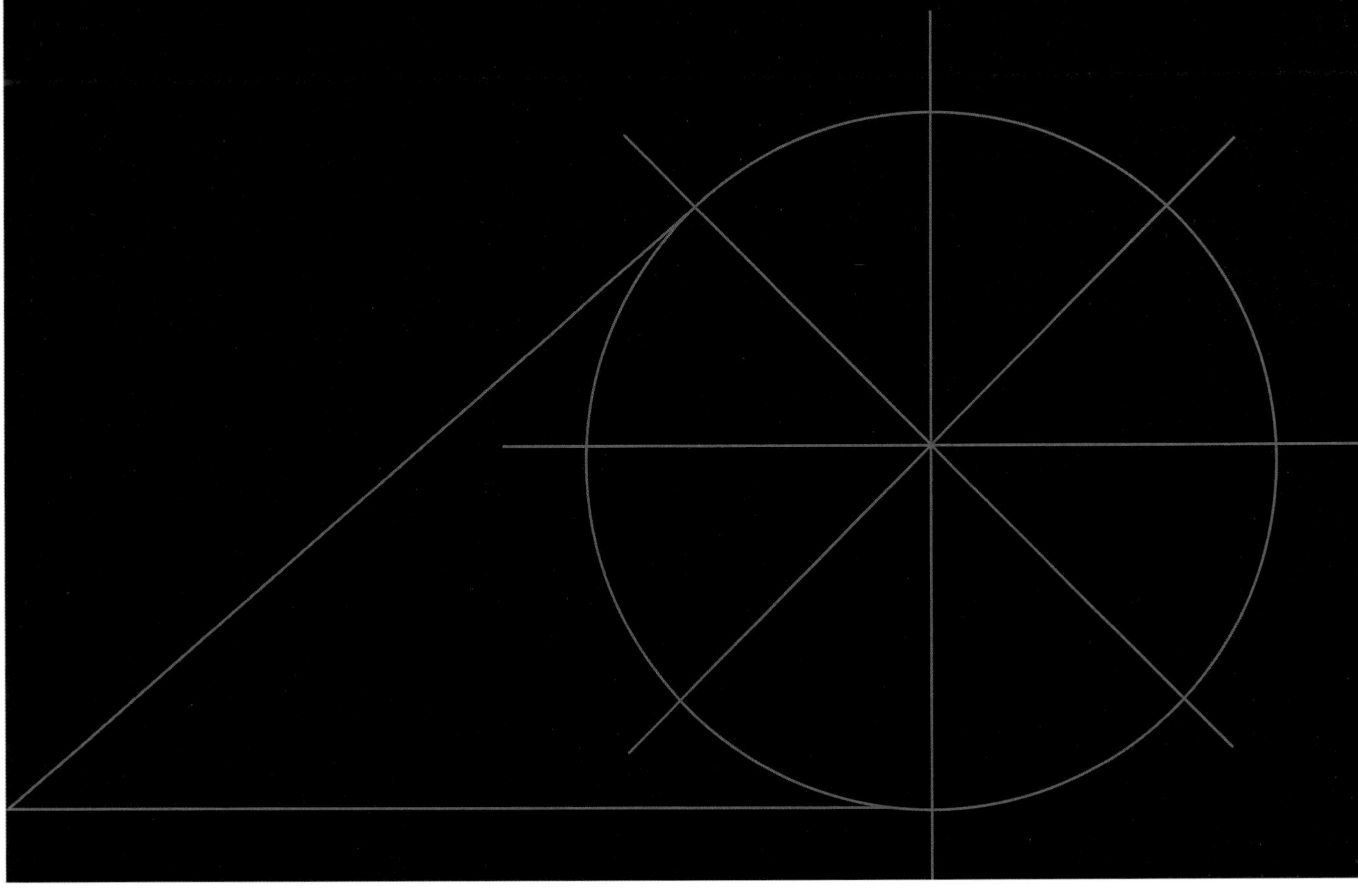

For Gandhi, freedom from British rule was not the end. It was only the beginning of an effort to build a new India. He held that real *swaraj* would come through constructive programmes which could be called the construction of *purna swaraj* by non-violent and truthful means which would help in achieving 'independence of every unit, be it the humblest of the nation, without distinction of race, colour or creed.'

Visiting a riot affected area of Jahanabad, Bihar, March 1947

All Men Are Brothers

Speaking at a public meeting in Rangoon in 1929, Gandhi said—

> my mission is not merely freedom of India... but through realisation of freedom of India I hope to realise and carry on the mission of brotherhood of man. My patriotism is not an exclusive thing. It is all embracing and I should reject that patriotism which sought to mount upon the distress or exploitation of other nationalities.[82]

Gandhi wanted Indians to respect other religions just as they respected their own. 'Mere tolerance, he said was not enough.'[83]

All religions, according to him were different roads converging to the same point. 'What does it matter that we take different roads so long as we reach the same goal?'[84]

Inter religious prayer for communal harmony, 1946

'When you look at these religions as so many leaves of a tree they seem so different, but at the trunk they are one.'[85]

'Every formula of every religion has in this age of reason, to submit to the acid test of reason and universal justice if it is to ask for universal assent. Error can claim no exemption even if it can be supported by the scriptures of the world.'[86]

Gandhi held that Indian society was pluralistic, that Indian civilisation was committed to pluralism as a desirable goal; not just a collection of different ethnic, religious and cultural groups, but unity in diversity. It was an open civilisation with permeable boundaries allowing new influences to flow in and vitalise the old. As Gandhi had observed, over the centuries, Indians had blended with one another with the utmost freedom and made India a

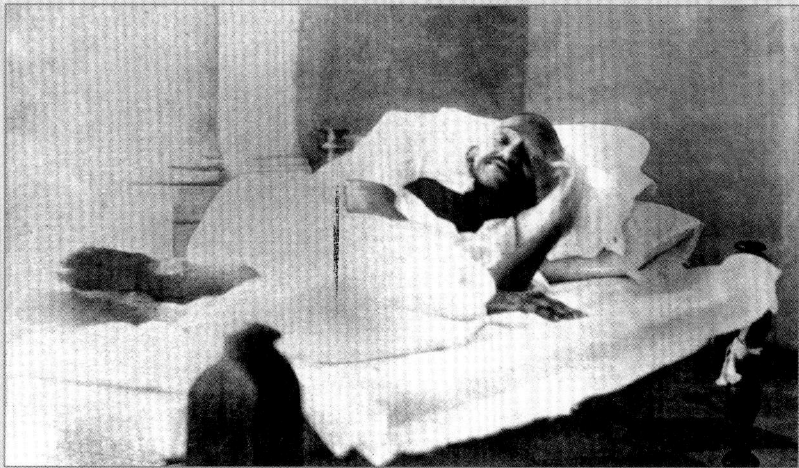

Fasting for Hindu-Muslim Unity, 1924

microcosm of the world. Our civilisation is a synthesis of different cultures. It was neither Hindu, Muslim nor Christian but a fusion of all of them. He held that each of us may catch a glimpse of some aspect of truth, but it is not possible for anyone to grasp the totality. Professor Karl Popper, author of *Open Society and its Enemies*, said that there was only one way to get to the truth—every argument should begin with the two contestants declaring, 'I may be wrong and you may be right.' Gandhi believed that no religion teaches intolerance. Everyone has his own truth, therefore, no one has the right to force others to abandon their truth in favour of yours. From this sprang his belief in tolerance.

FROM THE TOP

Discussing with Maulana Anwarulla, Noakhali, 1947

On the Peace Mission at Noakhali, 1946

FROM THE TOP

With Khan Abdul Ghaffar Khan, Bihar Peace Mission, 1947

At Gurudwara in North-West Frontier Province, 1938

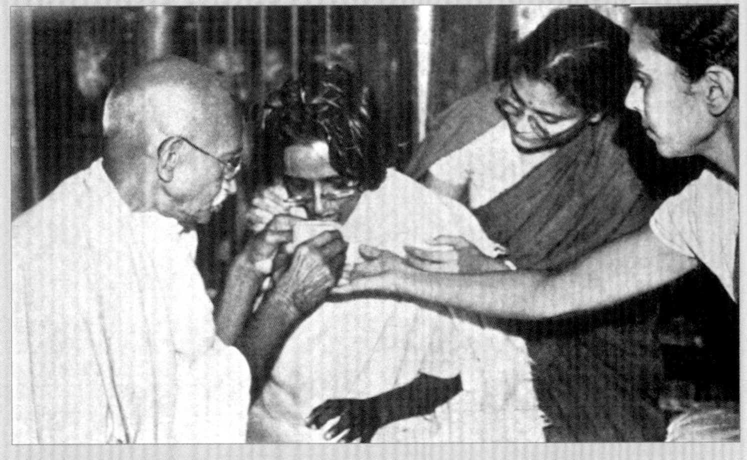

FROM THE TOP

Breaking the fast of Bibi Amtus Salam

At YMCA, Sri Lanka, 1927

All his life Gandhi worked against religious hatred and for communal peace and harmony. He regarded Hindu-Muslim unity as imperative and it was one of the central planks of his constructive programme. He was able to achieve this unity during the Khilafat/Non-Cooperation Movement. Towards the end, this became his mission and a cause for which he finally laid down his life. He went from village to village in Noakhali and from there to Bihar, and then to Calcutta to extinguish the flames of communal hatred.

But Gandhi's idea of pluralism extended beyond Hindu-Muslim unity. In November 1921, during the visit of the Prince of Wales to Bombay riots broke out when Congress and Khilafat volunteers attacked Parsis and other minority groups who had welcomed the Prince's visit. Over fifty people died and hundreds were injured. Gandhi was deeply disturbed and went on a fast to calm the situation. Throughout his career he made efforts to reach out to all communities. He tried to reassure Parsis of his commitment to minority rights. Towards the end of the Non-Cooperation Movement, he adopted the formula of 'Hindu-Muslim-Sikh-Parsi-Christian-Jew' unity.

He firmly believed that people of all religions, languages, colours and creed could live peacefully and had done so for centuries in India. 'Love has no boundary. My nationalism includes the love of all nations of the earth irrespective of creed.'[87]

CURSE OF UNTOUCHABILITY

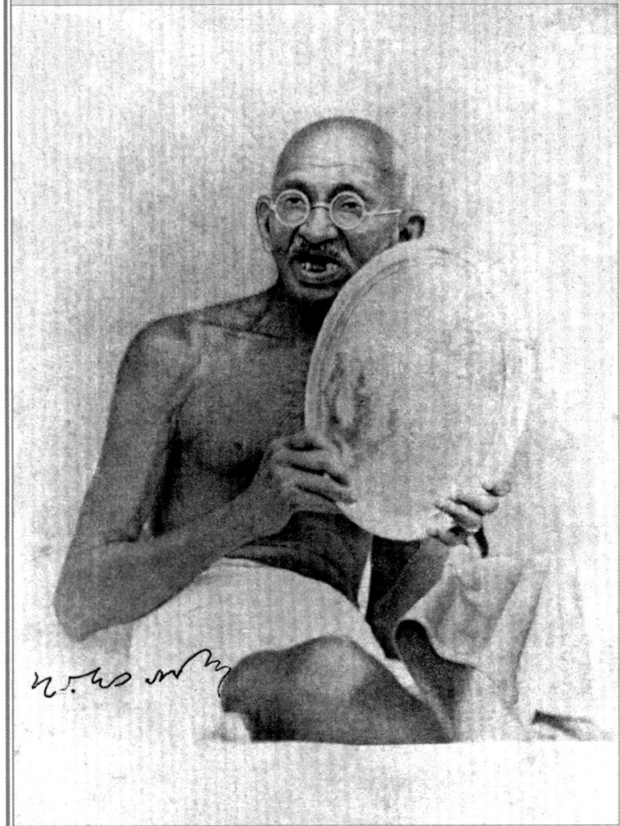

Gandhi said that the love of the people for him brought the problem of untouchability early into his life. To Ambedkar, he wrote,

> I know that you have drunk deep of the poisoned cup. However, I make a claim that will astound you. You are born an untouchable but I am an untouchable by adoption... I learnt the lesson of democracy at the tender age of 12. I quarrelled with my mother for treating the domestic sweeper as an untouchable. That day I saw God in the form of a Bhangi. You spoke the truth when you said that the welfare of untouchables is dearer to you than my own life...[88]

He held that *swaraj* would be a meaningless term, if we keep a fifth of our population under perpetual subjection and deny them the fruits of national culture. For reform of Hinduism and for its real protection, removal of untouchabilty was essential. Untouchability was a soul destroying sin. 'I would rather that Hinduism died than that untouchability lived.' For him, it was a wholly artificial product. It had no connection with the intellectual or moral development of people.[89]

With Thakkar Bapa, Secretary, Harijan Sevak Sangh, 1935

FACING PAGE Auctioning a silver plate for collecting Harijan Fund

LEFT TO RIGHT

Collecting money for Harijan Fund, 1934

Mobilising the masses, 1934

Inaugurating a common well for all, 1933

Having a meal together—with people with all castes, 1933

FACING PAGE (FROM THE TOP)
Addressing to the people during Harijan Tours, 1934
While overseeing an inter-caste marriage at Sevagram Ashram, 1940

Noakhali Peace Mission, 1947

After his return to India from South Africa, Gandhi set up his first ashram at Kochrab near Ahmedabad. He laid down nine vows for the ashramites, among which was non-observance of untouchability. He admitted an untouchable family— Dadabhai, his wife Daniben and their daughter Laxmi— into the ashram. The inmates of the ashram, including Kasturba, were unhappy and avoided contact with this family. If they entered the kitchen, they cleaned

Discussing ways to maintain peace and harmony, Delhi, 1947

and scrubbed it. At his prayer meeting, Gandhi announced that those who could not accept the untouchable family could pack up and leave. He was prepared to give up his wife for the sake of his principles.

> In battling against untouchability and in dedicating myself to that battle, I have no less an ambition than to see a complete regeneration of humanity. It may be a dream and as unreal as the silver in the sea-shell. It is not so to me while the dream lasts, and in the words of Romain Rolland, 'Victory is not realisation of the great, but in the relentless pursuit after it'[90,91]

Kasturba and others are spinning the *charkha*

Vision of India as a Stable, Flourishing and Sustainable Nation

POLITICAL AND SOCIAL STRUCTURE

Gandhi held that a government always functions through the implicit consent of the people. It simply cannot function when the people oppose it outright.[92] 'Self-government necessarily means government by the free and intelligent will of the people.'[93]

Real *swaraj,* he said, will come 'not by the acquisition of authority by a few but by the acquisition of the capacity by all to resist authority when it is abused.'[94]

He believed that every human being has the right to live, and therefore, to find the wherewithal to feed himself and where necessary to clothe and house himself.[95]

According to him, the economic constitution of India, and for that matter, of the world should be such, that no one under it should suffer from the want of food and clothing.

With Kasturba, 1931

In other words, everybody should be able to get sufficient work to enable him to make the two ends meet.[96]

'That economics is untrue', he said, 'which ignores or disregards moral values. The extension of the law of non-violence in the domain of economics means nothing less than the introduction of moral values as a factor to be considered in regulating international commerce.'[97]

He was not against the use of machinery per se. However, he did not want machines to displace the labour of those who cannot otherwise be employed.[98]

According to him, it was not nationalism that was evil. 'It was the narrowness, selfishness, exclusiveness which is the bane of modern nations which is evil.'[99] No culture can live, he said, if it attempts to be exclusive.

'I do not want my house to be walled in on all sides and my windows to be stuffed. I want the culture of all lands to be blown about my house as freely as possible. But I refuse to be blown off my feet by any.'[100]

Gandhi held that poverty dehumanises human beings, undermines their sense of dignity and self-respect, wastes their potential and deprives their lives of all meaning and purpose. It is one of the worst forms of violence that human beings can commit against other human beings. It is as bad as killing and even worse for the fact that it is silent, slow and invisible, arouses no anger, and is outside the purview of anyone's direct responsibility.

As long as even one person is starving and lacks decent housing, the social order stands indicted. The first duty of the state and society is to provide the basic human needs. God, he said, comes to the poor in the form of bread.

> I will give you a talisman. Whenever you are in doubt, or when the self becomes too much with you, apply the following test. Recall the face of the poorest and weakest man whom you may have seen, and ask yourself if the step you contemplate is going to be of use to him. Will he gain anything by it? Will it restore him to a control over his own life and destiny? In other words, will it lead to swaraj for the hungry and spiritually starving millions? Then you will find your doubts in yourself melt away.[101]

Gandhi wanted to identify himself with the poor in India and so he took to wearing a loin cloth, minimising his wants, living in a mud hut and eating the simplest food. In South Africa, he had taken the vow of voluntary poverty.

Gandhi believed that 'a semi-starved nation can neither have religion, nor art, nor organisation … whatever can be useful to starving millions is beautiful to my mind … let us give today the vital things of life and the graces and ornaments of life will follow.' His mission in life, he said, 'was to wipe every tear from every eye.'[102]

In one of his newspaper columns, Gandhi reproduced some pithy quotations sent in by a 'fair friend'.[103] These include what have come to be known as Gandhi's *Seven Social Sins*. They are: Politics without principles, Wealth without work, Pleasure without conscience, Knowledge without character, Commerce without morality, Science without humanity, and Worship without sacrifice. These and many of his other writings show that, for Gandhi, economics together with politics, morality and religion formed an indivisible whole.[104]

Gandhi on his way to a public meeting, 1935

Gandhi receiving a silver casket, 1933

FACING PAGE (FROM THE TOP)
Gandhi addressing a public meeting, 1935
Gandhi addressing a public meeting, 1946

Nehru addressing a meeting with Gandhi

FACING PAGE Visiting the Physical Institute, 1927

With Jawaharlal Nehru and co-workers, 1935

He was deeply concerned about the disparities in our society between the rich and the poor and the fact that inequality destroyed the spirit of the community. This is the same inclusive growth about which economists, social scientists and politicians are talking today.

Gandhi was against large scale industrialisation. He advocated small and medium sized industries, localised production of food and clothes and agro-industrial units based in villages. Some of these ideas may not be applicable in today's world, but their underlying principle is important and we need to find appropriate means for realising it.

After independence, Gandhi's ideas of village based economy were not accepted on the ground that it could not generate enough resources to end poverty and make up for the backlog of India's underdevelopment of centuries. However, the emergence of new tensions and dangers in the affluent societies today are inducing a mood of introspection and sending us back to Gandhi.

ECOLOGY AND ENVIRONMENT

At the turn of the millennium, one of the central questions facing us is to preserve, protect and ensure the safety and stability of our planet. Depletion of the ozone layer, global warming, land degradation, deforestation, drying up of water resources and loss of biodiversity all are grave threats to our very existence.

The use of fossil fuels is increasing by leaps and bounds. The use of many other non– renewable resources is increasing at a mind boggling rate. The use of renewable resources of land, water, biomass, etc. is also increasing in a most unsustainable manner.

Gandhi had grasped the grave consequences of greed based economic pursuits, limits of technology and dangers of consumerism. His famous dictum that 'the earth has enough for everyone's need but not for everyone's greed' is today regarded as the basis of equitable and sustainable development. One should know one's own capacity and as the saying goes, 'You should stretch yourself according to the length of your bedspread.'[105]

The world today is becoming more and more concerned of the dangers to human life as a result of climate change caused among other things by air and water pollution, deforestation, etc. In India, open defecation is another problem; Gandhi said long ago that the construction of toilets was more important than building temples. He said that sanitation was one of the most important things which a humanitarian or a reformer must tackle. 'Every educated Indian has the unique privilege;' said Gandhi, 'he can become a missionary in hygiene and sanitation.'[106]

'Air is free to all, but if it is polluted, it harms our health. Doctors say that this bad air is more harmful than bad water.'[107]

'God forbid that India should ever take to industrialism after the manner of the West. The economic imperialism … is today keeping the world in chains. If an entire nation of 300 millions took to similar economic exploitation, it would strip the world bare like locusts.'[108]

'Nature has provided us with sufficient reserve of vitality. But for that man would have long ago disappeared from the face of the earth because of his own mistakes and transgressions of the rules of health.'[109] He held that conservation of forests, systematic plantation of trees, irrigation and many other things cannot be properly done without a common policy.[110]

For Gandhi, cleanliness was next to godliness. 'We can no more gain God's blessings with an unclean body than with an unclean mind.'[111]

Gandhi said that the cause of many of our diseases was the condition of our lavatories and our bad habit of throwing excreta anywhere and everywhere.[112]

'We are all children of the earth and it is only if we keep our vows that we can live on this earth preserving our self-respect.'[113]

'*Ramanama* also stood for the natural and right way of living.'[114]

'Nature Cure implies that the treatment should be the cheapest and the simplest possible.'[115]

'The naturopath recognises physical, mental and spiritual ills and treats them mainly by developing inner powers.'[116]

'Nature cure connotes a way of life which has to be learnt; it is not a drug cure as we understand it.'[117]

'Today we permit heaps of garbage to be in front of our homes and thus feed the disease and the doctors.'[118]

At the annual session of the Congress, 1927

Gandhi at a public meeting, 1938

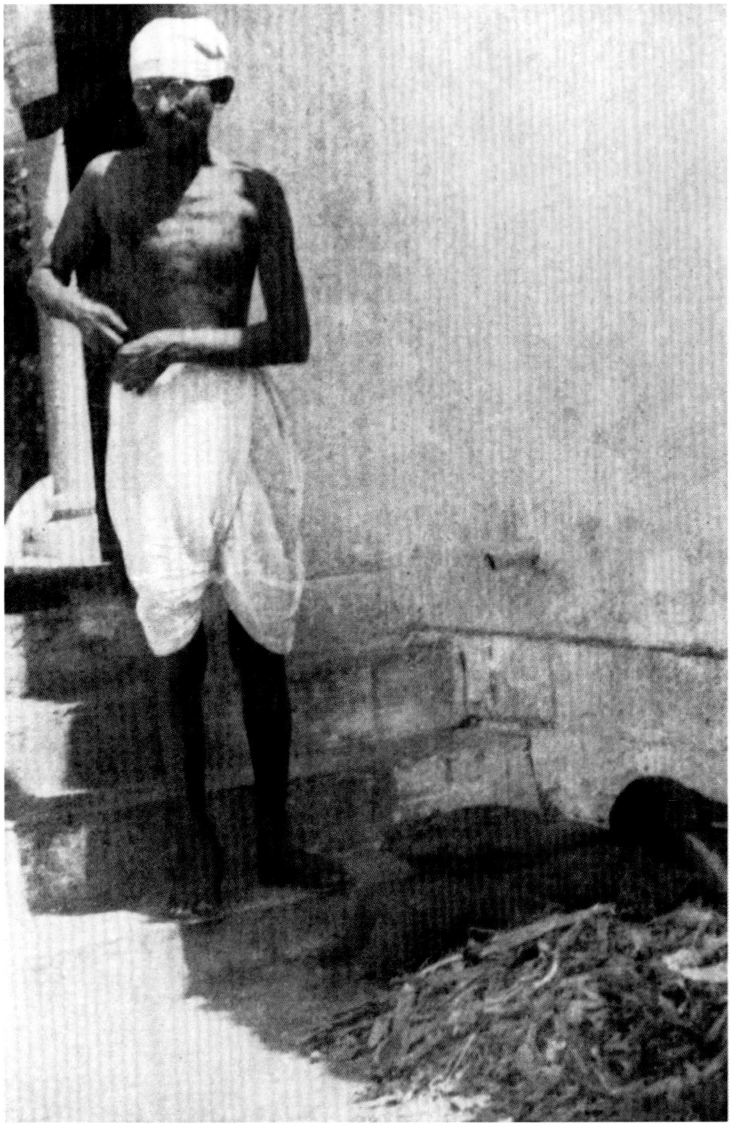

Ready to clean up the garbage, 1936

LEFT TO RIGHT

Gandhiji planting a tree, Sevagram, Maharashtra, 1941

Observing the process of compost making at the Institute of Plant Industry, 1934

Instructing the village cleaning squad, 1939

Caring for a growing plant

Sanitation campaign at community level

Gandhi with J.C. Kumarappa and others, Sevagram, Maharashtra

Fundamental lesson of cleanliness

FACING PAGE Mahatma Gandhi in the banana garden, Sevagram, Maharashtra, 1941

Boys and girls from Ahmedabad taking part in spinning

Progress with Knowledge and Education

The primary aim of all education, he said, is or should be character building. In a letter to his son Manilal, written from Volksrust prison in 1909, Gandhi wrote, 'Education does not mean a knowledge of letters but it means character building.' He distinguished between literacy and knowledge and held that literacy in itself was no education. Development of human personality was far more significant than the accumulation of intellectual tools and knowledge. He envisioned true education coming about primarily through a particular pattern of life in a community and not merely through formal instruction in schools. Schools should prepare citizens of a society– a non-violent society– and teach children to live on the basis of co-operation, truth and *ahimsa*.

The essential tenets of education as propounded by Gandhi can be summed up as follows:

FROM THE TOP
Presiding as Chancellor of Gujarat Vidyapith
Addressing school children, 1927

FACING PAGE With workers of Kheda, 1929

1) Education must serve the nation's needs consistent with the philosophy of freedom, truth and non-violence.
2) Equality of all religions and all men.
3) Equal importance to intellectual training and manual work, which should be socially useful and productive.
4) Mother tongue as the medium of instruction at all levels along with the compulsory teaching of Hindi.
5) The curricula and other arrangements should aim at serving the needs of villagers.

Classroom of Kishore Singhji Primary School where Gandhi studied

It was a basic principle of all Gandhian institutions that teachers should regard untouchability as a blot on Hindu society and should strive for its removal and should never exclude a boy or girl for reasons of his being an untouchable, nor treat him or her differently after admission.

Manual work was an integral part of Gandhian education. There is no point, he used to say, in developing the brain only. One has to develop one's brain through one's hands.

Gandhi had been engaged in the work of rural reconstruction, *harijan* uplift and political regeneration and therefore, his fingers were constantly on the pulse of the common people. He realised that unless education was given a new orientation, it would not be possible to build the social order that he cherished. He placed before the nation a scheme which he had been evolving for 40 years— a scheme popularly known as the Wardha Scheme of Education, which he called 'Nayee Talim' or New Education. He defined it as education for life and through life.

Gandhi's educational ideas grew out of his experiments in education with his family and in his *ashram*s in South Africa and India before they were formulated and publicly announced. By education he meant an all-round drawing out of the best in the child and man— body, mind and spirit.[119]

'That education alone is of value,' he said, 'which draws out the faculties of a student so as to enable him or her to solve correctly the problems of life in every department.'[120]

'*Nayee Talim* means teaching through craft. That basic craft has to be selected in the light of the conditions and produce of the region.'[121]

According to him, self-reliance was the most important characteristic of Nayee Talim. The knowledge that this

Weaving skill

FACING PAGE (FROM THE TOP)
Mass spinning, 1946
Learning through game

Education through music

system imparted could not be had from books. It was from nature that this knowledge had to be obtained. 'Knowledge directly derived from anything was much better than knowledge derived through a written lesson or through symbols. That was the essential basis of *Nayee Talim*.'[122]

Basic education discarded bookish learning and aimed at an all-round development of the child so that he could become a useful and productive member of the society. In his last talk on Nayee Talim on 14 December 1947, Gandhi said, 'Basic education is generally interpreted as education through craft. This is true to a certain extent, but this is not the whole truth. The roots of *Nayee Talim* go deeper. It is based on truth and non-violence in individual and collective life.'[123]

The Wardha scheme left out teaching of religion because Gandhi held that religions as they were taught and practised led to conflict rather than unity. Truths common to all religions could be taught. No denominationalism or factionalism was to be encouraged specially between Hindus and Muslims.

Independent India abandoned Gandhi's ideas on education. But today, once again, we are emphasising the importance of skill development and vocational education. Looking at the national scene, with growing violence, rape, crimes against women, *dalits* and minorities, increasing individual and corporate corruption, and lack of moral standards, one realises why Gandhi placed so much importance on character building as crucial for the nation building.

Developing the art of cooperation

FACING PAGE Education— the basic *mantra* of life

Mahatma Gandhi on the telephone, 1939

FACING PAGE Mahatma Gandhi reading a letter in a happy mood, Birla house, Mumbai, August 1942

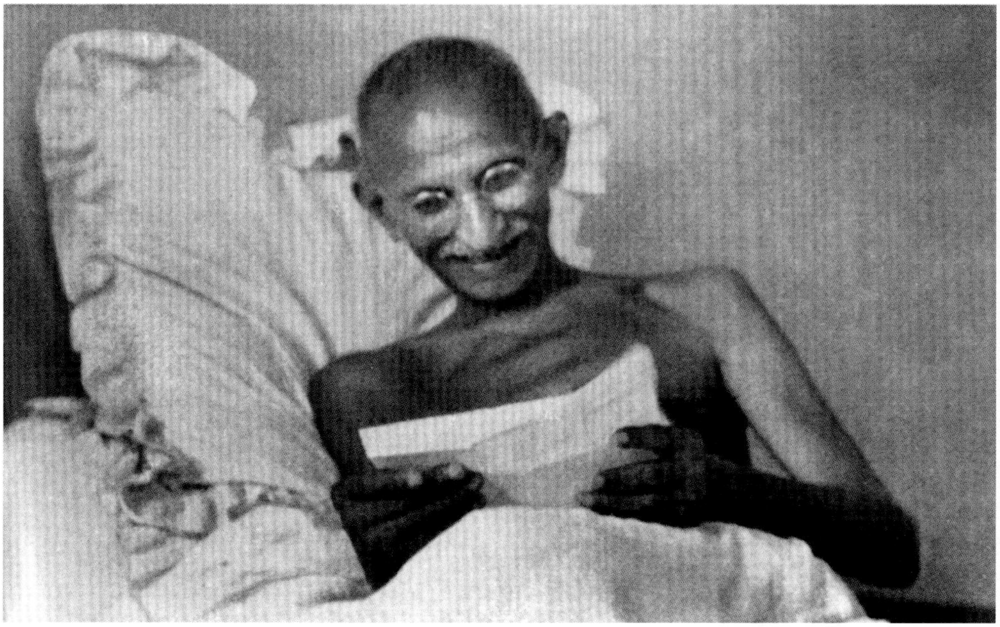

LANGUAGE OF LEARNING

'Our system of education has three aspects. It leads to the development of the mind, body and the soul.'[124]

JOY OF SHARING

Gandhi's life was one of constant experimentation to know the truth and to live it according to his light. This light never ceased to illuminate his awareness and to spread the luminosity among those with whom and for whom he worked. He had the gift to learn and grow with experience of events in daily life and the principles he held, evolved out of his experiences and experiments.

Gandhi's idea of the resolution of conflicts not by violent struggles between classes or castes or communities, but by peaceful, non-violent means, of removing poverty and inequality, of the 'small is beautiful', of preserving the environment, of honesty and probity in public life, of his belief in pluralism, of an open society and an open polity—are all extremely relevant today. The Prophet would have the vision of the Poet, of an India:

'Where the mind is without fear
and the head is held high;
Where knowledge is free,
Where the world has not been broken up into
fragments by narrow domestic walls;
Where tireless striving stretches its arms
towards perfection;
Where the clear stream of reason has not lost its way
into the dreary desert sand of dead habit;
Where the mind is led forward by thee into ever
widening thought and action—
Into that heaven of freedom my father,
let my country awake.'[125]

Walking alone

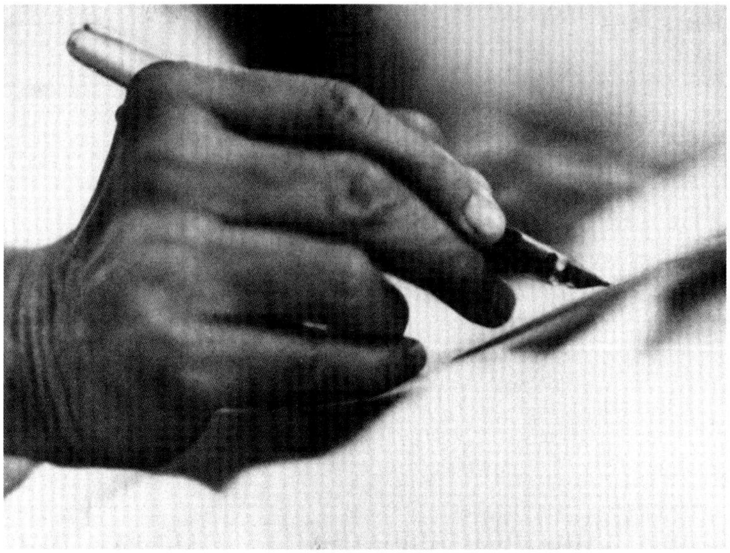

The creative hand

FACING PAGE Gandhiji reading a newspaper

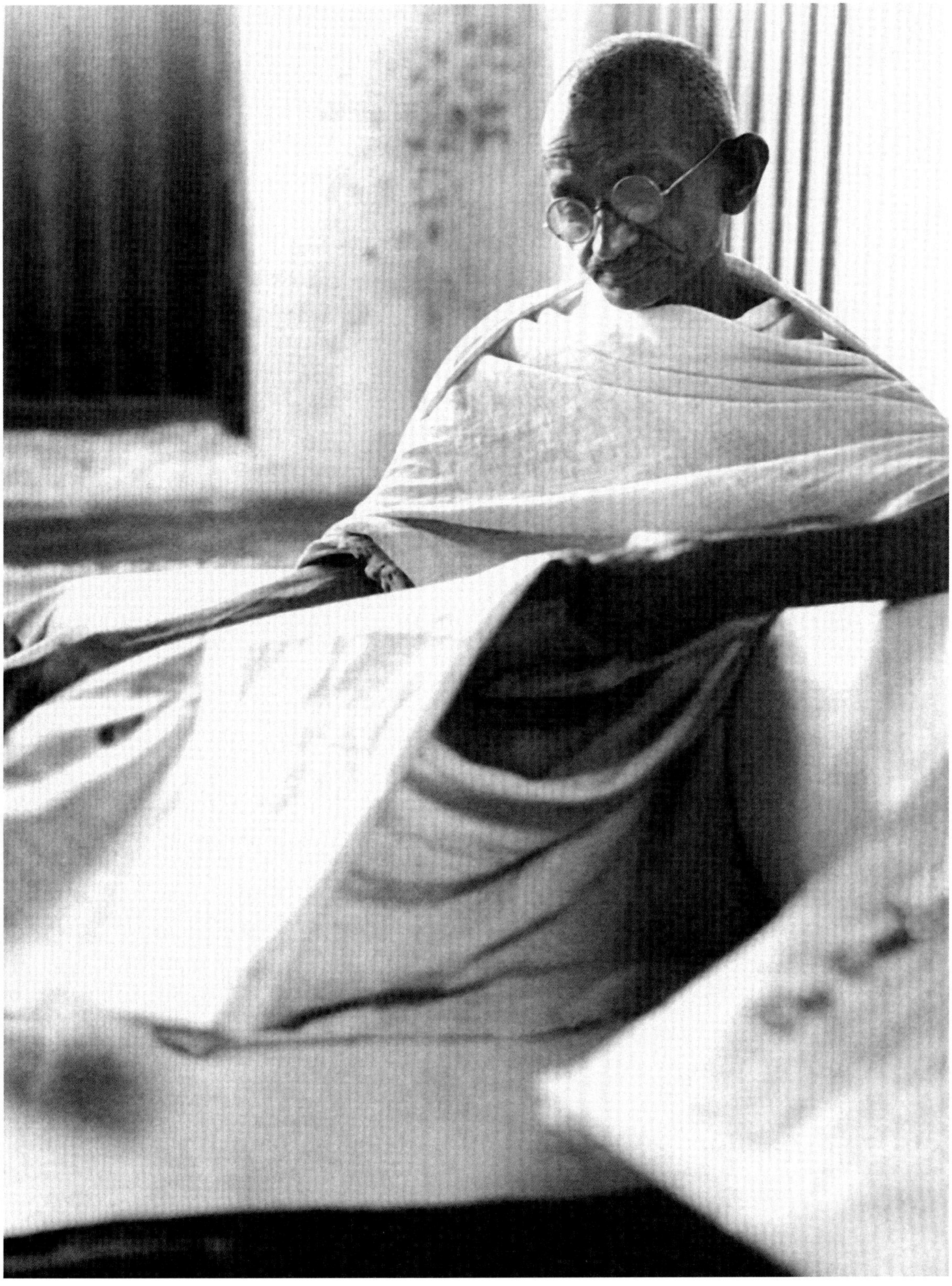

Gandhi and Kasturba having breakfast at Sevagram, Maharashtra

FACING PAGE Gandhi interacting children after a prayer meeting, Juhu, Bombay (now Mumbai), May 1944

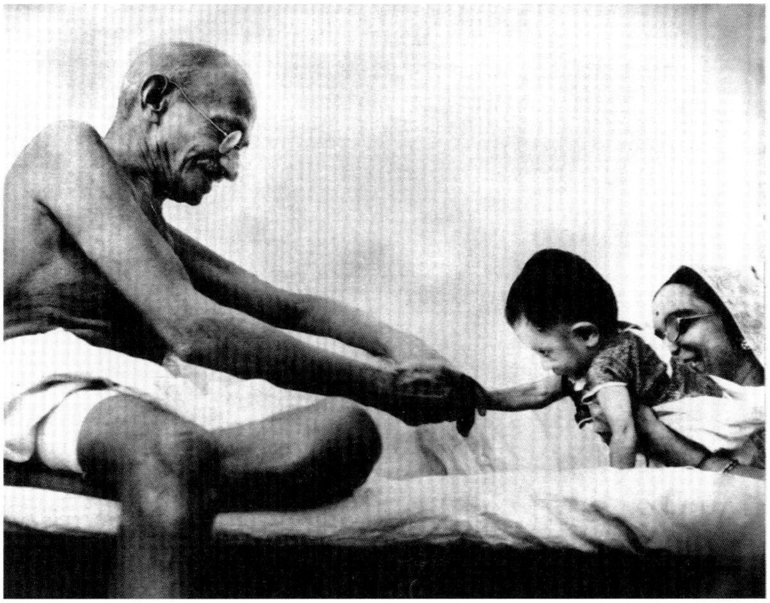

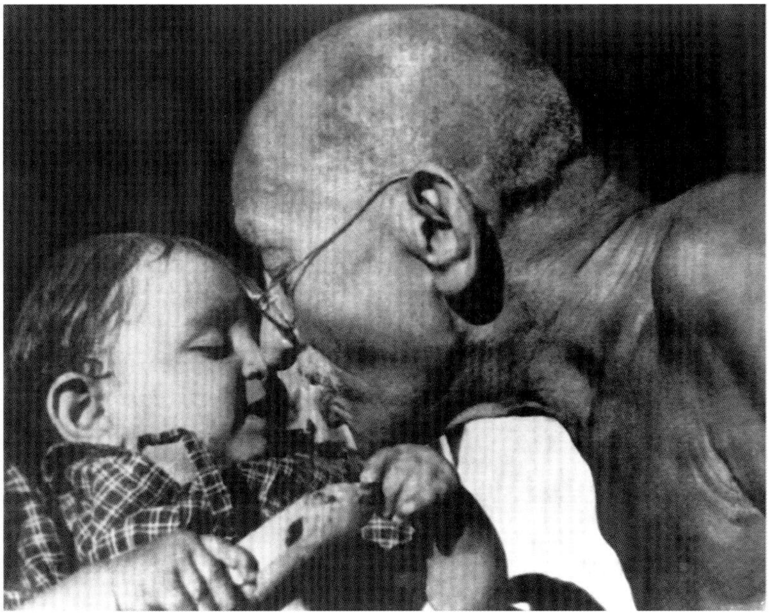

Gandhi and Hingorani with a child on the occasion of a birthday ceremony, Sevagram, 1944

Mahatma Gandhi with others during his Assam visit, January 1946

Mahatma Gandhi, 1938

Acknowledgements

I am deeply grateful to the National Gandhi Museum for their support and help. In particular, I would like to thank Anupama Srivastava, photo section-in-charge, Nilam Rani, assisant editor, and Mokshda Sharma, PA to the Director. Anupama, for providing the photographs, Neelam for the captions, and Mokshda for proof reading the entire manuscript and checking the references. I would also like to thank Shri Padmanabhan, the librarian, and Ms Deepali, the assistant librarian for tracing books and references. Shri Annamalai, Director, National Gandhi Museum supervised the entire project. I would also like to thank Niyogi Books for the excellent design and layout, and Arunima Ghosh and Mohua Mitra for providing editorial assistance, reading the manuscript and giving their very useful suggestions. Without the cooperation and assistance of them all, this book could not have been written.

Mahatma Gandhi spinning a wheel, 1947

References

1 Bipan Chandra, *The Epic Struggle*, Orient Longmans, 1992, p.2.
2 Ramin Jahanbegloo, 'The Dream He Had,' *The Hindu*, 3 April 2018.
3 Lynn Burnett, 'African Americans Make Contact with Gandhi,' *Article of The Cross Cultural Solidarity History Education Project, Histories of black/brown solidarity, black internationalism, white allyship, and struggles against white supremacy*, http://crossculturalsolidarity.com/african-americans-make-contact-with-gandhi-the-1930s.
4 Kinga Rodkiewicz, 'Civil Disobedience in Poland, its roots and examples,' Satyagraha/Civil Disobedience, *Article of Bombay Sarvodaya Mandal and Gandhi Research Foundation*, https://www.mkgandhi.org/articles/civil_dis.htm.
5 Václav Havel, *Power and Powerless: Citizens Against the State in Central Eastern Europe*, M.E. Sharpe, 1985.
6 N.S. Bose, *Indian Awakening and Bengal*, Firma K.L. Mukhopadhyay, Calcutta, 1960, p.154.
7 Quoted in Charles Heimsath, *Indian Nationalism and Hindu Social Reform*, Bombay, Oxford University Press, 1964, p.16.
8 M.K. Gandhi, *Satyagraha in South Africa*, Navajivan Publishing House, Ahmedabad, Vol. 19, p.109–10.
9 M.K. Gandhi, *Collected Works of Mahatma Gandhi*, Publications Division, Ministry of Information and Broadcasting, Government of India, Vol. 8, p.36–8.
10 K. Gopalaswami, *Gandhi in Bombay*, Bombay Gandhi Smarak Nidhi, Bharatiya Vidya Bhavan, 1969, p.22.
11 M.K. Gandhi, *An Autobiography Or The Story of My Experiments with Truth*, Navajivan Publishing House, Ahmedabad, 1948.
12 Ibid.
13 Gilbert Murray, *Hibbert Journal*, 1918, cited in D.G. Tendulkar, *Gandhi in Champaran*, Publications Division, Government of India, restored edition 2017, p.114.
14 Erik H. Erickson, *Gandhi's Truth: On the Origins of Militant Nonviolence*, London, Faber and Faber Ltd 1970, p.351.
15 Ibid.
16 M.V. Kamath and V.B. Kher, *The Story of Militant Non* Violent *Trade Unionism, A Biographical and Historical Study*, Navajivan Trust, Ahmedabad, 1993, p.132–3.
17 Rajmohan Gandhi, *Patel: A Life*, Navajivan Publishing House, Ahmedabad, 1992, p.58.
18 M.K. Gandhi, 'Statement to Disorders Inquiry Committee,' *The Collected Works of Mahatma Gandhi*, Vol. 19, 5 January 1920, p.206.
19 Bipan Chandra, Mridula Mukherjee, Aditya Mukherjee, Sucheta Mhajan and K.N. Panikkar, *India's Struggle for Independence*, Penguin Random House India, 1988, p.188.
20 Idem.
21 Prabhudas Gandhi, 'Recalling Memories of 1921,' *1921 Movement: Reminiscences*, Foreword by V.V. Giri. Publications Division, Government of India, 1961, p.77–87.
22 Sumit Sarkar, *Modern India*, Macmillan, 1983, p.213.
23 M.K. Gandhi, *Young India*, 2 March 1921.
24 Bipan Chandra, *Indian National Movement: The Long Term Dynamics*, Har Anand Publications, New Delhi, p.46.
25 Ibid. p.47
26 Mahadev Desai, *The Story of Bardoli: Being a History of the Bardoli Satyagraha of 1928 and its Sequel*, Navajivan Publishing House, Ahmedabad, 1929, p.42–43.
27 M.K. Gandhi, *Collected Works of Mahatma Gandhi*, Publications Division, Ministry of Information and Broadcasting, Government of India, Vol. 36, p.73.
28 M.K. Gandhi, *Collected Works of Mahatma Gandhi*, Publications Division, Ministry of Information and Broadcasting, Government of India, Vol. 43, p.2–8.
29 Ibid. p.3.
30 Anil Dharker, *The Romance of Salt*, Roli Books Pvt. Ltd., New Delhi, 2005, p.7.

31 Ibid. p.25.

32 Prajabandhu, 25.5.1930; 11.5.1930 cited in Aparna Basu, 'Gujarati Women's Response to Gandhi, 1920– 1942', *Sammya Shakti*, Vol. 1, No.2, 1984, p.10.

33 Anup Taneja, *Gandhi, Women and the National Movement, 1920– 47*, Har Anand Publication, Delhi, p.123.

34 Durgabai Deshmukh, Oral History Transcript, Nehru Memorial Museum and Library, p.32.

35 Kamaladevi Chattopadhyaya, *Inner Recesses Outer Spaces*, Niyogi Books, New Delhi, 2014, p.149– 51.

36 Usha Thakkar and Sandhya Mehta, *Gandhi in Bombay*, Oxford University Press, 2017, p.160.

37 Ibid. p.161.

38 Ibid. p.165.

39 Ibid. p.163.

40 Ruchi Seth, *Women's Response to the Freedom Movement: A Case Study of Delhi*, Unpublished M.Phil. Thesis, University of Delhi, 1991, p.51– 52.

41 Vishalakshmi Menon, *Indian Women and Nationalism, The U.P. Story*, New Delhi, Shakti Books, 2003, p.81.

42 J. Nehru, *Discovery of India*, Meridian Books, London, 1946, p.303.

43 Webb Miller, *I Found No Peace*, The Literary Guild, New York, 1936, p.193– 94.

44 Thomas Weber, *On the Salt March*, Harper Collins, India, 1997, p.444– 445.

45 Kamaladevi Chattopadhyaya, '*The Struggle for Freedom*' *in Women in India*, Publications Division, Ministry of Information and Broadcasting, Government of India, 1958, p.19– 20.

46 Anil Dharker, *The Romance of Salt*, Roli Books Pvt. Ltd., New Delhi, 2005, p.116.

47 Parshotam Mehra, *A Dictionary of Modern Indian History, 1707– 1947*, Oxford University Press, New Delhi, 1985, p.573.

48 M.K. Gandhi, *Collected Works of Mahatma Gandhi*, Publications Division, Ministry of Information and Broadcasting, Government of India, Vol.76, p.377– 381.

49 Ibid, p.384– 396.

50 Ibid, p.391– 2.

51 *Harijan*, 26 July 1942.

52 Rina Pal, *Women of Midnapore in the Indian Freedom Struggle*, Rana Prakashan, Calcutta, 1996, p. 88– 93.

53 Usha Thakkar and Sandhya Mehta, *op.cit.*, p.257– 258.

54 Aparna Basu, *University of Delhi, 1927– 1997*, p.43– 44.

55 Bipan Chandra, Mridula Mukherjee, Aditya Mukherjee, Sucheta Mahajan and K.N. Panikkar, *India's Struggle for Independence*, Penguin Random House India, p.461– 463.

56 Lakshmi Menon, ed. Roshni, February 1946, All India Women's Conference, Lucknow, p. 3.

57 *Tribune*, 18.2.146. cited in Anup Taneja, Gandhi, Women and the National Moverment, 1920– 1947, Har Ananad Publications, New Delhi, 2009, p.190.

58 Geraldine Forbes, *Women in Modern India*, Cambridge University Press, South Asian Paper Back edition, New Delhi, 1998, p.208.

59 Bhashyam Kasturi, *Walking Alone, Gandhi and India's Partition*, Vision Books, New Delhi, 1999, p.55.

60 M.K. Gandhi, *Collected Works of Mahatma Gandhi*, Publications Division, Ministry of Information and Broadcasting, Government of India, Vol. 85, p.295.

61 *Harijan*, 2 March 1947, *Collected Works of Mahatma Gandhi*, Publications Division, Ministry of Information and Broadcasting, Government of India, Vol. 87, p.34.

62 *Harijan*, 9 February 1947, *Collected Works of Mahatma Gandhi*, Publications Division, Ministry of Information and Broadcasting, Government of India, Vol. 86, p. 451.

63 M.K. Gandhi, *Collected Works of Mahatma Gandhi*, Publications Division, Ministry of Information and Broadcasting, Government of India, Vol. 87, p.206.

64 B.R. Nanda, *Mahatma Gandhi*, London, Allen and Unwin, 1958, p.495.

65 M.K. Gandhi, *Collected Works of Mahatma Gandhi*, Publications Division, Ministry of Information and Broadcasting, Government of India, Vol. 86, p.166.

66 Mridula Sarabhai, *Gandhi in Bihar 1946– 47 and National and Emotional Integration*, Calico Museum of Textiles, Ahmedabad, 2005, p.9.

67 Ibid.

68 Ibid.

69 Ibid. p.13.

70 Manu Gandhi, *The Miracle of Calcutta*, Navajivan Publishing House, Ahmedabad, 1959, p.21.
71 *Statesman*, 13 August1947, cited in *Kasturi*, 105.
72 Bhashyam Kasturi, *Walking Alone, Gandhi and India's Partition*, Vision Books, New Delhi, 1999, p.105.
73 Manu Gandhi, *The Miracle of Calcutta*, Navajivan Publishing House, Ahmedabad, 1959, p. 29–30.
74 Philip Zeigler, *Mountbatten*, Collins, Lonson, 1985, p.436.
75 *Statesman*, 15 August 1947, cited in *Kasturi*, p.108.
76 *Gandhi's Correspondence with the Government, 1944–47*, Navajivan Publishing House, 1969, p.277.
77 Pyarelal, *Mahatma Gandhi, The Last Phase*, Navajivan Publishing House, Ahmedabad, 1956, Vol.2, p. 415–415.
78 Ibid. p.421.
79 Bhashyam Kasturi, *Walking Alone, Gandhi and India's Partition*, Vision Books, New Delhi, 1999, p.112.
80 *Statesman*, 1 Septermber 1947, cited in *Kasturi*, p.113.
81 M.K. Gandhi, *Constructive Programme: its Meaning and Place*, Navajivan Publishing House, Ahmedabad, p.8.
82 *Amrita Bazar Patrika*, 10 March 1929.
83 M.K. Gandhi, *Collected Works of Mahatma Gandhi*, Publications Division, Ministry of Information and Broadcasting, Government of India, Vol. 78, p.391.
84 Ibid. Vol. 10, p.29.
85 Ibid. Vol. 72, p.254.
86 Ibid. Vol.26, p.202.
87 Raghavan Iyer, *The Essential Writings of Mahatma Gandhi*, Oxford University Press, 4th ed. 1996, p.245.
88 Mahadevbhai Diary, Vol. 1, *Collected Works of Mahatma Gandhi*, Publications Division, Ministry of Information and Broadcasting, Government of India, Vol. 51, p.458–460.
89 Ibid, Vol. 57, p.306.
90 *Young India*, 26 November 1931, p.372.
91 Gopal Gandhi, *The Oxford India, Gandhi*, Oxford University Press, New Delhi, 2008, p. 344–5.
92 M.K. Gandhi, *Collected Works of Mahatma Gandhi*, Publications Division, Ministry of Information and Broadcasting, Government of India, Vol. 18, p.56.
93 Ibid. Vol. 76, p.402.
94 Ibid. Vol. 26, p.52.
95 Ibid. Vol. 13, p.312.
96 Ibid. Vol. 37, p.411–412.
97 Ibid. Vol. 25, p.475.
98 Ibid. Vol. 41, p.511.
99 Ibid. Vol. 27, p.255.
100 Ibid. Vol. 29, p.159.
101 *Mahatma Gandhi: The Last Phase*, Vol. 11, 1958, p.65.
102 M.K. Gandhi, *Collected Works of Mahatma Gandhi*, Publications Division, Ministry of Information and Broadcasting, Government of India, Vol. 33, p.93.
103 *Young India*, 6 August 1925.
104 Thomas Weber, *The Mahatma, His Philosophy and his Legacy*, Orient Blackswan, Hyderabad, 2018, p.138.
105 M.K. Gandhi, *Collected Works of Mahatma Gandhi*, Publications Division, Ministry of Information and Broadcasting, Government of India, Vol. 63. p.402.
106 Ibid. Vol. 5, p.101.
107 Ibid. Vol. 14, p.143.
108 Ibid. Vol. 38, p.243.
109 Ibid. Vol. 77, p.5.
110 Ibid. Vol. 28, p.458.
111 Ibid. p.462.
112 Ibid. Vol. 27, p.154.
113 Ibid. Vol. 63, p.403.
114 Ibid. Vol. 84, p.29.
115 Ibid. p. 203.
116 Ibid. Vol. 58, p.304.
117 Ibid. Vol. 83, p.218.
118 Ibid. Vol. 75, p.352.
119 Ibid. Vol. 65, p.450.
120 Ibid. Vol. 62, p.436.
121 Ibid. Vol. 82, p.142.
122 Ibid. Vol. 83, p.53.
123 Aparna Basu, 'Gandhi on Education,' paper written for Seminar on Gandhi and National Integration, October 1987, Vigyan Bhavan, New Delhi, organised by Gandhi Smriti and Darshan Samiti, New Delhi, p.7.
124 M.K. Gandhi, *Collected Works of Mahatma Gandhi*, Publications Division, Ministry of Information and Broadcasting, Government of India, Vol. 87, p.389.
125 Rabindranath Tagore, *Gitanjali*, Rupa & Co., New Delhi, 2003, Vol. 35, p.40.

Index